The Development
Practitioners' Handbook

D

The Development Practitioners' Handbook

Allan Kaplan

Pluto Press

LONDON • STERLING, VIRGINIA

First published 1996 by Pluto Press
345 Archway Road, London N6 5AA
and 22883 Quicksilver Drive,
Sterling, VA 20166–2012, USA

British Library Cataloguing in Publication Data
A catalogue record for this book is available from the British
Library

ISBN 0 7453 1020 6 hbk
ISBN 0 7453 1021 4 pbk

A catalogue record for this book is available from
the Library of Congress

Designed and produced for Pluto Press by
Chase Publishing Services, Sidmouth EX10 9QG
Typeset from the author's disk by
Stanford DTP Services, Towcester
Printed in the European Union by
Antony Rowe, Chippenham, England

Contents

FOR SUSAN
Something to read on the way

...he loved the desert because there 'the wind blew out one's footsteps like candle-flames'. So, it seems to me, does reality. How then can we hunt for the truth?...

Indeed, now the masters were beginning to find that they were, after all, the servants of the very forces they had set in play, and that nature is inherently ungovernable.

Lawrence Durrell, *The Alexandria Quartet*

Acknowledgements

How does one trace the genesis of an idea, the genealogy of one's evolving questions and tentative stabs at an answer? How can one specify the profound influences which colour the warp and weft of one's thoughts? There are so many whom I would acknowledge; I have been in debt since my earliest years.

Some, however, deserve particular gratitude with respect to this work. All of my colleagues at CDRA, both board and staff, have been integral to the development of this book. Also, the development practitioners who have shaped CDRA's practice: Hamo Hammond, Mario Van Boeschoten, Fritz Glasl, David Scott and Alan Fowler. I must thank in particular Dave Harding and Sue Soal, without whose valuable commentaries this work would have been far less intelligible. I must also thank Ben Parker and Hendrik Rabie, brothers whose perspectives, while often contrary, have served to hone my own thinking even while challenging my certainties. To Valda West, whose creativity and devoted professionality with respect to wordprocessing is unsurpassed, I offer humble thanks. Also to Roger van Zwanenberg, whose confidence as a publisher enables me to develop confidence as a writer.

I must also thank my father, who led me into his beloved mountains and opened me to journey and essence and good argument. I thank my children, through whom I have assumed the mantle of leadership in a very particular sense. Most of all I have been blessed by Susan, lover, friend, wife and mentor whose depth of love is matched only by the honesty of her striving to consciousness and her unflagging enthusiasm about the journey.

Preface

Development is recognised as a major challenge, if not *the* major challenge, facing us all as we move towards the twenty-first century. There is no question, however, that those who practise development do so within a terrain which has become highly contested and contentious. On the one hand we know that the schisms and inequities which characterise relationships between individuals, communities and nations are tearing at the fabric of social life and beginning to render it untenable. Therefore for many years both the nations of the West and of the North – the so-called developed nations – as well as those of the South and of the East – predominantly the so-called underdeveloped nations – have been struggling with different ways of conceptualising and understanding development, and of intervening in socioeconomic and political processes in an attempt to achieve greater equity, justice and social coherence (not to mention, more recently, ecological stability). On the other hand we know too that little has been achieved in this regard during the last three to four decades of what has come to be known as the development era. There are many, both within 'underdeveloped' communities themselves as well as amongst development theoreticians and practitioners, who have come to question, and even scorn and ridicule, the very notion of development.

Thus after more than 30 years of international development practice and theorising, problems of unemployment, housing, human rights, poverty and landlessness are worse than ever. Frans Schuurman, in an exploration of development theory at an 'impasse', notes that 200 years ago the income ratio between the world's rich and poor countries was 1.5:1; in 1960 it was 20:1; in 1980, 46:1; and in 1989 it reached a high of 60:1[1] World Bank figures show that the number of people living below the minimum poverty line (US$1 a day) in Africa, for example, increased from 68 million in 1982 to 216 million in 1990.[2] Viewed from a slightly different angle, rich nations give about US$60 billion in aid to developing countries while earning US$125 billion in compensation from military expenditure out of these same countries.[3] Small wonder then that Wolfgang Sachs and colleagues, in a damning and articulate indictment of development, note that 'the idea of development stands like a ruin in the intellectual landscape'; they maintain that the development epoch is crumbling under the weight of delusion, disappointment, failure and crime, and that 'the time is ripe to write its obituary.'[4]

They are right, of course, but only partially so, and they offer few alternatives to the predicament in which we find ourselves. Anger and cynicism, when they engender only despair, are of limited assistance. We are where we are, caught between a rock and a hard place, between paradigms and between competing worlds, and opting out holds as little promise as does continuing along the same path with blind resolution. We need to explore the contradictions in our understanding and in our practice of development in order to move beyond this impasse.

I have worked as a development practitioner for some years now, and, even in the face of these contradictions, I have developed a profound respect for the development process as a reality and as a path of human striving. I have come to believe that we have limited the potential of development intervention by constraining our understanding of the phenomenon within socioeconomic and political parameters. We have thus reduced our perspectives rather than expanded them. We have diminished the notion of development from a reality of life itself to a measure of our own paltry stature. Vaclav Havel has noted that '...it is strange but ultimately quite logical: as soon as man began considering himself the source of the highest meaning in the world and the measure of everything, the world began to lose its human dimension, and man began to lose control of it.'[5]

This work will attempt to expand our current understanding of development and to look at the concept from new, various, and, hopefully, helpful perspectives. I have no wish to capture development within a quote, or within a theory or set of irrevocable laws. The concept is integral to life itself, and as such cannot be caught, dissected or explained; neither can it be explained away. We can observe, we can describe, but we cannot fix. Goethe said, in his attempt to understand the nature of colour, that 'It is really vain to attempt to express the nature of something. We notice effects, and a complete account of these effects would perhaps comprise the nature of this thing. We attempt in vain to describe the character of a man; but a description of his actions and his deeds will create for us a picture of his character.'[6]

I would like to examine development with this in mind. To be authentic in our attempt to understand development, to be true to the concept itself, we need to respect our own developing, and, therefore, inconclusive understanding; we need to acknowledge the fact that development is itself a life process, and therefore never static or complete. We cannot hope to describe and understand the life of a river by focusing on the analysis of a glass of water.

This work will hopefully be of use to people working in the field, actively doing development work. In this rocky place in which development practice finds itself, there is little to guide development practitioners in their actual development practice, despite many of the learned treatises which have been written on the subject. And, as we have seen, there is much that is dubious that goes under the name of development. Academic theoreticians do not seem to help the practitioner much. Neither does the project manual, which assumes that causal sequences will create clear steps which lead to logical consequences. Life – and development – is not like that. We cannot treat it as if an articulate theory plus a step-by-step guide will lead to a finished product. To take from Havel once more, from his 1992 speech to the World Economic Forum in Geneva, the belief that the world is controllable and that we will control it as soon as we have discovered the ultimate theory, is precisely the kind of thinking which generates the crises we face.[7] Our belief in analysis, in the mechanistic world view, in the technological fix, has generated crises which cannot be solved by the means which created them. We need to release life from the confines of our technical intellect; we need to restore respect, imagination, ambiguity and awe for the life-force itself.

I shall argue in this work for the recognition of the development practitioner as a professional, a necessary and important professional, with a disciplined body of knowledge to draw on. I shall argue that the discipline of the development practitioner is an art, one which demands imagination, flexibility and the ability to work with ambiguity and contradiction; one which works with living people and life processes; one which can use guidelines but not rules; one which demands humility and respect in the practitioner; and one which is inherently creative rather than technical, while at the same time being grounded within an accessible and rigorous framework.

I shall contend that the art is one of facilitating the growing consciousness of others, and therefore one which demands continual effort at self-development on the part of the practitioner. Given the facilitative nature of the art, I shall explore, as well, where the development practitioner is best placed to pursue his or her work. In order to achieve the above, and to remain true to the living nuances of development, I shall be looking at development from the point of view of the individual, the organisation, the community and society, as well as a living process in its own right.

To come close to the essence of the concept of development, we must undertake a journey of exploration. This work is neither an attempt to produce a manual on the techniques and various methodologies of development practice; nor to rationalise the indefensible. Rather, it is an attempt to pursue the illusive nature of development itself, in order to deepen, to underpin, the practice of development; to provide it with a foundation and a meaning. (Such an investigation will necessarily raise both concepts and philosophical spheres of argument which I shall not pursue beyond what is necessary for the integrity of the current discussion. This project releases potentially debilitating complexities; I shall endeavour to maintain accessibility by focusing on core meanings.)

In all my work with development practitioners I have come to recognise that, with the best of them, the 'tricks of the trade' are of secondary importance. A prerequisite for effective practice is the approach, the understanding, the perspective and the value-base, out of which the development practitioner operates. What follows is an attempt to explore essentials.

Prelude: A Mountain Community

Years ago, before realising that development practice is an art and discipline in its own right, and before recognising the development practitioner as a professional, I went as a community worker to 'do development work' in a remote mountain community. I went, or was sent (as most community workers are sent) with little understanding of my role and even less support, relying on intuition and the arrogant presumption that I knew more than those I was sent to 'serve' there. I had no training in community work as such, nor was this expected of me for those who sent me assumed – as do many NGOs (non governmental organisations) even today – that community development work was an ad hoc and informal non-discipline in which one bumbled along hoping to find one's feet, or not as the case may be. Since leaving that community, in which I lived for three years, I have striven to understand the development practitioner's art and to gain recognition for the development practitioner as a disciplined professional whose work is not only vital but also, I believe, profoundly consequential with respect to humanity. I have worked with urban and rural organisations of civil society; with national and regional organisations throughout Southern Africa; with northern donors and with development practitioners from many countries. I have gained experience and reflected actively on that experience. Years later, I think back on my experiences in that mountain community with gratitude, appreciation and love, and realise in retrospect that time contained great learnings for me; that the kernel of my developing practice was formed then; and that my quest has, in a sense, been an endeavour to understand the dilemmas and uncertainties of that time. I shall therefore intersperse the chapters of this book with interludes about that time and that community, with vignettes which might serve to bring the body of the text closer to home.

Wupperthal is situated in the Cedarburg mountains, 300 kilometres north of Cape Town. It consists of a central village with twelve 'outstations', or smaller villages, many scattered in remote valleys where access is difficult. It is an area inhabited – during the days of apartheid South Africa, which is when these incidents occurred – by poor, disenfranchised, coloured people who had once been labourers on white-owned farms.

Wupperthal was founded in the early 1800s by German missionaries. The missionary church has since become an independent South African church and still owns the land and, in a real sense, the people. The majority of Wupperthal residents are subsistence farmers, although some farm on an economic basis (rooibos tea, small stock farming) and certain small industries have been established including a glove factory, shoe factory, tannery and village shop. However, in the face of declining economic viability and urban migration, the church was at a loss as to how to maintain and develop the community. I was sent in, partly to do research, partly to establish cooperative ventures, using current farming and 'industrial' activities as the basis for development.

Wupperthal is a beautiful, timeless place, remote and isolated. The mountains are harsh and uncompromising; the lines on the faces of the people seem to take on the character of the weather-beaten rocks themselves. The people are closely connected to their land, their crops, animals, and their community. They have little else. They live a life which cycles with the seasons. They welcomed me into their midst with open arms – but as a person, not as a development worker. Their understanding of my role was fraught with inconsistency, as indeed was my mine.

From the first I was confronted with dilemmas. The church had sent me in, yet there was little love between the church and the people. In spite of employing me to undertake development work, the church confounded every effort which I made or which the people made to develop themselves. From its head office in Cape Town the church appeared to wish to maintain the villagers' dependence and subservience. And for many reasons the people were apathetically antagonistic to the church. I found I was caught in between.

The people themselves had little interest in the changes which appeared to be the inevitable consequences of the development process. They had no wish to change their subsistent, timeless way of life; they had not asked for me to come in. At the same time, they were no longer a contented community. Their poverty hurt, and many younger community members were migrating to the cities. The money which they sent back to their elders was beginning to create social divisions between the haves and have-nots. Division had never existed before when all had only 'what God had the grace to give us'. The people resisted change, yet were patently unhappy with their current state.

I found my position ambiguous. Development seemed necessary, yet should I force development on an unwilling people? The irreverent nature of their response to my efforts and their resistance to change made me wonder whether I could, let alone should, facilitate development. The people were asking for my assistance all the time, yet continuously resisting the implications of that assistance for their lifestyle. Was development necessary? Perhaps my interventions were disturbing the integrity of village life, and I should leave the situation to evolve or gradually disintegrate on its own.

What would development bring anyway: a TV set to replace a winter's fire in the hearth? A formica kitchen table to replace the roughly hewn cedarwood table? Yet people were suffering, and at their wit's end.

I walked the mountains, and my questions bounced back at me from cliff faces and ricocheted down tumbling kloofs.

1

Natural Processes

Observations Concerning Biological, Human and Organisational Development Processes

...I had seen birth and death, but had thought they were different; this birth was hard and bitter agony for us, like death, our death...

T.S. Eliot, *The Journey of the Magi*

A small rural community in the mountains was my point of departure, and it remains the starting point for these reflections. Not for investigating development work as such, but rather for beginning a journey of exploration into the concept of development itself. For 'out there' humanity is given its proper measure as merely one factor in a vast and powerful panoply of life. In the mountains it is nature which impresses; the processes of birth and death, evolution and dissolution, development over time. Peaks rear their thrusting heads, rocks erode and crumble, water whittles valleys through eons of activity. And the worlds of plant and animal are enmeshed in an interweaving and symbiotic expression of the forces of life. One is forced to take note, to go beyond the constraining presumption that the concept of development is a variable primarily of political, economic or social life. Development is taking place all the time, all around, and we form a strand in the web rather than the scope by which it is assessed.

To give development its due one cannot start with analysis, with a breaking down into component parts or with theoretical hypotheses. The most important faculty in any intervention, be it to understand or to change, is the faculty of observation. Particularly observation which is embracing. To really observe in an unbiased fashion will allow us to experience the effects of development as they manifest around us, and so

1

approximate a penetration of development itself. Thus, before we analyse, before we theorise, let us try to simply observe the living process of development as closely as we can.

This is itself, perhaps, our primary observation. We can learn about development through observing it as a life process; more specifically as a biological process. Dale Harris noted, in his book *The Concept of Development,* that development is fundamentally biological.[1] What can we learn from observing biological processes?

We should recognise before beginning, however, that development as a biological process is not simply and linearly transferable to development as a socioeconomic or organisational process. Human beings are not purely determined by the laws which govern processes of biology; with people, the element of choice enters the picture, and they are thus also able to determine. Nevertheless, we too are subject to life processes which go on beyond us and which are embedded in the very fabric of our lives. Therefore we look to biological processes partly as indicators of the workings of development and partly as metaphors to assist in characterising development more clearly. Put another way, we are partly using the biological references here as a heuristic tool to better grab hold of the stuff that development is made of.

Bernard Lievegoed, in his highly original and seminal work *The Developing Organisation*[2] – to which I am indebted for many of the insights which follow – names the biological process of unfolding as 'maturation', an inevitable ripening towards an end which is preordained, towards which the organism is predisposed. A form of 'blueprinted development'. Whereas human and social development is the subject of choice, of intentionality, and is therefore not in any sense predetermined. Yet in biological, human and organisational processes of unfolding, similar patterns can be observed, and can be used to deepen our understanding.

Development in Biological Process

The first observation to note is the distinction between growth and development. These two concepts are often conflated, but they are not the same thing at all; growth is in fact one element of development. Growth is quantitative increase; development implies qualitative increase and qualitative transformation (from one state to another). Growth describes a change not of the 'thing' itself but only of one of the variables (quantity). Thus, growth depicts a quantitative increase within the same basic structure, while development depicts a change in the whole structure of the system itself. In other words, when an organism (system) grows quantitatively, it reaches a point at which its increased size can no longer be held together by its original structure, and restructuring of the organism is necessary. This restructuring of the entire organism (system) is an essence of development. The metamorphosis of caterpillar to butterfly is one obvious example of the transformation of structure and the birthing of an almost entirely new organism.

Lievegoed goes on to point out other aspects of the biological development process. For instance, we observe that development is a process in time. This might perhaps seem so obvious as to be insignificant, if not irrelevant. But it is a vital observation, for it should bring with it the correct attitude towards developmental processes – that of respect and humility. Development needs time, and flows with the rhythm of time. It cannot be forced, imposed or created. This is not to say that we cannot affect it; indeed, the development practitioner must seek to influence the process of development.

But the appropriate stance becomes one of facilitation rather than force; nurture rather than imposition; respect rather than arrogant presumption. We cannot cause development; we can only nurture the development process. Processes occur which will follow their own pace, undetermined by our own presumptuous interference. The wisest of those dealing with living processes recognise the integrity of the pace at which maturation unfolds. Leo Tolstoy in *War and Peace* reflects that apples should not be picked while green; they will fall off themselves when ripe but if an apple is plucked unripe the apple is spoilt, the tree is harmed, and one's teeth are set on edge.[3]

Development, or maturation, implies an unfolding in time, and this unfolding always takes place in what may be termed a forward direction. This reveals another distinguishing characteristic of development: it is irreversible. The irreversibility of almost all natural phenomena is a basic fact of experience. We know that we cannot grow younger (biologically speaking, at least), that we cannot make a river flow uphill, that it is impossible to fit the fully grown tree back into the seed from which it came. Paul Davies, an eminent scientist and philosopher, notes that the universe as a whole is engaged in unidirectional change, from past to future, and that 'most physical processes that occur in the real world are irreversible'.[4] Development is irreversible because it is, in fact, this very process of forward moving change. To use a previous observation, once the structure has changed, it cannot revert to its previous form and still continue to grow. If reversion does take place then we have not been witness to a development process.

Coupled with irreversibility comes another observation: that development is never 'instead of' but always 'as well as'. In other words, when an organism or system changes its structure, it is not that the previous structure is jettisoned, rather the previous structure is incorporated into the new. Each step in the process of development is gathered (transformed) into the next. One can thus trace in the evolution of biological forms and processes the imprint, or background pattern, of structures, forms and processes which have come before. We can begin to read biological history, evolutionary process, the story of maturation and unfolding, in that which we study. Nothing is lost, nothing was pointless or irrelevant; everything 'old' is transformed and used in the building of the 'new'.

A further aspect of development is the concept of differentiation and organ formation (sub-system formation), whereby functions initially carried out by the system as a whole are now concentrated in sub-systems and thereby made more effective. Thus development leads to more complexity as one system is differentiated into a number of systems, all of which need to work together to maintain the adequate functioning of the entire organism. Forward movement always entails differentiation or the separating out of simple systems, or organisms, into a complex multitude of specialised sub-systems. The simple organism becomes more and more complex as life progresses; the history of life on earth bears eloquent testimony to this observation. Development, then, moves from the simple to the complex; from the homogenous unit to the differentiated system.

Following on from differentiation comes the concept of hierarchisation: certain differentiated organs, or sub-systems, are governed by others in order to ensure their optimal interdependent functioning, that is, to ensure that they work together. The danger inherent in differentiation is that different specialised sub-systems begin to operate independently of each other, perhaps to their own short-term gain but to the detriment of the larger system of which they form a part. Thus together with increasing complexity comes the need for self-organisation if the organism is to sustain itself. And self-organisation implies some form of hierarchisation whereby certain systems coordinate groups of sub-systems. (The term hierarchisation often has negative associations in the social sphere where it carries with it the connotation, and implication, of power and discrimination. This should not confuse or sidetrack us here; issues of power are in no way implied here or necessarily entailed. In any case, we are at the moment trying to observe what is, rather than valuing it or judging what should or ought to be.) Complexity and self-organisation are complementary concepts, both being necessary to power the forward movement of life. As with their partner concepts of differentiation and hierarchisation.

Differentiation and hierachisation are brought together in the concept of integration: as an organism differentiates and develops specialised sub-systems the process of hierarchisation allows a new system to be formed of greater complexity than the original. Were differentiation to take place without subsequent integration the entire system would simply fragment, with sub-systems performing in isolation. Hierarchisation is a method for achieving integration in the face of, or from out of, differentiation. In the unfolding movement of life, the patterned sequence appears to be division (differentiation) followed by organisation (hierarchisation) followed by cohesion or coherence (integration) at a new level or form.

Not only does this pattern clearly appear in biological science, but most areas of what is coming to be known generically as 'the new science' seem to come to the same conclusion: that life is a progression from the simple to the more complex; that increasing complexity brings with it not simply the necessity but indeed the very possibility of 'higher' levels of system being able to organise themselves; that inherent in complexity is differentiation and division; that self-organisation implies some form of hierarchy leading to integration. That the ability of life to develop ever more elaborate structures and functions, to evolve and adapt to a changing environment, is a function of these patterns which lie at the heart of the developing world.[5]

There is a further important element to observe within the patterns which we have been considering above. Contrary to what we often take for granted, the process of unfolding, the movement of life as maturation or development, is discontinuous. It proceeds in a stepwise fashion rather than in a smooth, continuous 'upward' motion. It proceeds, in fact, from structural crisis to structural crisis. Put another way, an organism (system) does not develop continuously but remains, for varying lengths of time, at a particular stage of development until growth (for example) causes structural crisis. At this point it makes a quantum leap and 'jumps' – differentiates into a model of greater complexity – and integrates into a new level of development. (It is not only growth which causes such crises. The common tick, for instance, will lie dormant in an embryonic state for many years until the right animal 'triggers' the jump to its matured form.) The organism will remain at the level of development it has thus attained until it arrives at the next crisis.

This brings us into contact with chaos theory, another field of research within the new science. It appears that what are called 'far-from-equilibrium open systems'[6] – in other words, systems in chaos – have a natural propensity to seek out higher and higher levels of organisation and complexity. Put differently, the movement towards higher levels of organisation and complexity – the movement of maturation and development – is conducted from out of chaos; it is facilitated by the state of chaos. Whatever state has been attained needs to be shattered so that, in the resulting chaos, rigidity can be broken down to allow for the forces of creation to enter and fashion, out of the resulting void, a new form or state at a new level of development.

Development, then, proceeds in leaps and bounds interspersed with periods of dormancy. Its line is staggered and lurching, rather than smooth and linear. We can observe this process not only in the natural world around us but in the process of evolution itself. Evolution, as the ultimate development process, has been characterised by the paleontologist Stephen Gould as proceeding in leaps, from crisis to crisis, in a discontinuous rather than in a continuous fashion.[7]

Development as Human Unfolding

As has already been noted, we cannot unequivocally or entirely transfer the 'maturation metaphor' to the human being as person (rather than organism); other factors such as freedom, choice and intentionality come into play. Nevertheless the process of human development displays similar patterns in its unfolding. As hunters have tracked animals through the African bush by reading their spoor since time immemorial, we can begin to learn the script which development leaves imprinted on individual histories and journeys. Freedom is always exercised within, and against, the parameters of constraint. Taking from the description, by the French biologist Jacques Monod,[8] of nature as an interplay of chance and necessity, perhaps we can say that humanity is an interplay of choice and necessity.

With people, too, development is a process in time. We have all had experience of things taking place in their own time, of certain times being more appropriate than others, of the relevance of different interventions for different times in a life's journey. Development, also, is a discontinuous process. In working with people who are moving through or confronting development processes, we observe the extreme resistance to change which people manifest. Reflecting on their own development over time, people notice that they tend to remain at a particular levels of development which are only shaken up at particular times, for example at significant life turning points which are not readily identifiable without intense reflection. We tend to resist change and development even in the face of a painful reality at a particular stage in our lives. And mostly, in order to make the next developmental leap, a crisis is necessary; a crisis large enough to make the previous stage of development no longer tenable.

An obvious and, currently, ubiquitous example of human development containing the patterns referred to above is the dissolution of a marriage. Always painful and more often than not resisted with incredible tenacity, it heralds despair and generally signals unbearable loss. Even when all is clearly lost it is almost impossible to reach the place within oneself which will accept the 'failure' as a stepping stone to something beyond. We 'fall asleep' into a particular reality and cannot imagine survival outside it, for there is nowhere else to go. Yet the forcing of passage through crisis can bring one to a surprising level of insight and understanding; a new, more resolute self can resurrect itself from the ashes. How else other than through critical turning points can we shake ourselves out of our comfortable habits, overcome our resistance to change and move on? This, I believe, is what is sometimes referred to as the miracle of suffering.

Development is not so much the pain of taking on the new but the pain of letting go the old. We all know how difficult it is to change unconscious habits and patterns and to let go. We have so much vested in who we are, and so much fear of walking naked into the future. In counselling people through development processes, the difficulty of letting go becomes the major challenge to be overcome. We cling to old structures and to old ways of being even when they no longer work.

There is another facet to the difficulty of letting go: we have no way of knowing what the new stage holds in store for us. Although we may have been told by others, we cannot ourselves have experienced it and therefore cannot know it. Fear of how we will perform in an unknown future is a large component of the resistance to change. Another component is the fear of loss. Every development process implies loss – the loss of the previous way of being. However dysfunctional that way of being may have become, it is known and habitual and therefore comfortable despite, or within, the pain which accompanies it. It implies too a more complex reality, as the development process moves from more simple to more complex states which present new challenges, generate new responsibilities, and require fundamental shifts in attitude and behaviour. In terms of the dissolution of a family, for example, life often becomes far more complex as a result of the shifts which take place. There are the ambiquities and uncertainties of 'blended families' to deal with; ongoing relationships with ex-spouses; children coming and going from one home, one family culture, to another; confusing issues around finance and responsibility.

Development, then, implies a paradigm shift, a new way of seeing the world. The phrase 'paradigm shift' comes from Kuhn's analysis of the development of science in *The Structure of Scientific Revolutions*.[9] It applies equally well to the concept of development on the individual and social level. Kuhn argues that science has progressed by a series of revolutions and not, as frequently supposed, by some orderly and continuous series of logical arguments and accumulating evidence. Each revolution was precipitated by a crisis in current thinking, and introduced a whole new way of thinking, of perceiving and of behaving. The word 'paradigm' represents a whole cluster of beliefs, values, theories and techniques. A significant change in such a paradigm is the prelude to a whole new set of efforts. (Thus, for example, the radical shift from seeing the sun as revolving around the earth to seeing the earth as orbiting the sun.)

The paradigm shift is the process of development as applied to thinking, to the realm of ideas. As previously seen, Gould has ascribed a similar process with respect to evolution; Lievegoed to the realm of biology, or processes occurring in nature. We have looked at the development process as it pertains to the life of the individual. If nothing else, these observations should serve to make us aware of, and respectful towards, development as a process which operates according to natural laws, laws which need to be worked with facilitatively rather than imposed upon with the customary arrogance which we often display towards the world around us. In working with development processes we work with the very stuff of life; it behoves us to be sensitive and imaginative and respectful without being passive. The development practitioner who works without love is like the proverbial bull in a china shop. Development practitioners should ideally serve and assist the processes of people's development. Yet we can so easily cause damage and hurt by forcing issues without understanding due process.

I have a friend who provides an illuminating example of these processes of individual development. He began his working life as a lawyer, and struggled for years in what was for him the straightjacket of that profession before breaking free to pursue the craft of pottery. This had always been his first love. He was a highly gifted and principled potter and followed in the tradition of the Japanese and English 'masters', even with respect to the type of clay that they used and the style of pottery they espoused. But despite dedicated hard work his products did not sell in his locality (the Western Cape Province of South Africa) and the stresses associated with this eventually took their toll on his physical and mental health.

As a result he changed his professional direction again, this time becoming a contracted fieldworker on a development project. But everything which could have gone wrong seemed to go wrong, and he sank into an even deeper depression. At the end of his contract he was relieved to go home, even though he felt he still had no solutions to the problems which had initially encouraged him to accept the field position.

But he had never entirely given up. On his return he experimented with new forms and new colours in his pottery and found that he achieved almost overnight success. He found that as he unshackled himself from the traditional paradigms in which he had formerly worked his true creativity was released. He began to work in clays which he had previously rejected, and came to recognise that his true artistry lay in the design and decoration process. As a result of this change he became recognised as a potter who had succeeded in creating new forms and possibilities for the craft, and his work was sought after, copied and admired. By taking a leap into the unknown, and by embracing the ambiguous relationship between tradition and innovation, he came through.

Elizabeth Kubler-Ross, having worked intensively with terminally ill patients, talks of five stages in the process of coming to terms with death.[10] The first response to the news is denial – there must be a mistake. Then bargaining – if I cut down on smoking can we presume this cancer to be treatable? When this does not work, anger takes its place – why me? Beyond this lies depression, and then, at the nadir of the void, acceptance. No more resistance. And strangely, this acceptance leads to new energy, rather than the opposite. And so much can be done with this new energy.

Every step taken in development, every process of transformation, entails a death so that something new can be born. And the process of death and rebirth, the process of development, entails the overcoming of just such resistances, so that new energy can be released.

Development as Organisational Dynamic

Many organisations seek an organisation development consultant for assistance when they face a crisis of some kind. In my consultancy work I am continually faced with the task of facilitating the client through crisis by helping that client to recognise that, while the crisis is certainly a danger and a threat, it is also a challenge and an opportunity for development.

As with the individual, the organisation tends to stagnate without crisis. Max De Pree has noted that all organisations tend towards stagnation, routine and unconsciousness, and consequently lose their cutting edge.[11] As with the individual, it is almost as if organisational life throws up crises in order to precipitate development. Life itself seems to function in the service of development.

The poet Pater wrote: 'Failure is to form habits.'[12] There is a terrible truth in these words. We are dependent on life distributing obstacles in our path in order to keep growing. Of course, we do not always need crises in order to grow, just as crises in themselves do not always precipitate development; we often fail to rise to the challenge, which is precisely where the development practitioner can make such useful interventions. Thus while crises are often the precipitators of development, nevertheless, unlike in the sphere of biological maturation processes, human and organisational development does not always imply 'development or death'. We can remain functioning at way below our potential for long periods, entire lives or generations in fact. Choice and consciousness differentiate human and organisational life from biological life.

Nevertheless, patterns similar to those described in biological and human development processes can be observed in the processes of organisational development as well. Crisis, as we have seen, plays a major role in precipitating development. Development is a process in time, and is distinct from growth. For here, too, growth implies quantitative increase, while development occurs when qualitative and structural transformation of the entire system takes place. As an organisation develops, the early homogeneity which characterises the nascent organisation is no longer sufficient to cope with its expanding reality; differentiation of tasks, functions and roles takes place, leading to sub-system formation and greater complexity. (In fact, the very word 'organisation' implies this aspect of development, for it implies 'organ formation' – the development of different sub-systems which typify the increasing complexity of the developing organisation.) As the organisation differentiates, the need arises for some form of hierarchisation: the coordination of the whole system by particular sub-systems in order to achieve integration in the face of increasing complexity. Without such integration, the system tends to fragment.

This is clearly seen when we observe particular organisations over time. I was asked to assist a large national organisation which was experiencing intense internal conflict and tension. The organisation had begun as a small family-type unit, led by a charismatic social entrepreneur. Most staff members could perform all of the necessary functions interchangeably, and intimate interpersonal relationships as well as interchangeable staff functions meant that there was no need for formal structures and procedures; decisions were made 'in the corridor', in an informal and ad hoc fashion, and there was no need for internal communication mechanisms as information was relatively uncomplex, and flowed freely between people whenever they bumped into each other. Ten years later the organisation had grown to over 100 staff members, there were branches in two other major cities and there were various specialised departments, such as administration, finance, media, fieldwork, training and research, which responded to the vastly increased complexity of each organisational function. Yet the organisation still prided itself on the informality and ad hoc nature of its decision-making processes and communication mechanisms. Organisational life was only deemed livable if informal personal contact was the sole means of regulating the system. But this was no longer possible. Each sub-system (departments and regional branches) had become small intimate organisations (teams) in their own right, and interdepartmental conflict was rife. Departments prided themselves on their independence, and worked more in the interests of their own specialisations than in the interests of the organisation as a whole.

Many changes had to take place in order to reduce conflict and tension and restore a healthy and competent working life. But perhaps the most important of these changes was the recognition of the need for, and the implementation of, formal coordinating structures and procedures which served to regulate the relationships between departments, decision-making, resource allocation and communication flow. Increasing formalisation and a form of hierarchisation – in the institution of a sub-system whose function was specifically that of coordination – reduced tension and conflict and allowed the sub-systems (departments) to work harmoniously towards the greater good of the organisation.

I present this example to illustrate points already made about differentiation, hierarchisation and integration as essential aspects of the development process. It illustrates other patterns as well. For instance, the concept of development as a process in time: the specific organisational intervention made, and the resultant developmental changes, could not have occurred sooner (or much later). Other patterns which the example illustrates and which have also been noted earlier include our natural resistance to change (our 'falling asleep into' routine and becoming unconsciously attached to habitual forms of behaviour even when they no longer actually work to our benefit) and the very real loss that goes with development. It was quite clear with this particular organisation that, while the development process had brought with it many essential benefits, it had also entailed the painful loss of informality, ad hoc decision-making, reliance on intimate interpersonal relationships and the human warmth which accompanied this. However, much of the warmth had already been lost to be replaced by conflict, and the 'coldness' of formal structures and procedures was necessary at this stage to restore not only organisational coherence but also sound human relationships. However, the sense of loss was real, as was the difficulty in letting go, and the uncertainty of the benefits of a more formal and structured future.

The above example serve to illustrate a further observation concerning the development process; an observation which is often hidden or avoided.

Pundits of development often assume that development is a panacea, that it is wholly good and that it is synonymous with peace, prosperity and neighbourly relations. Critics of socioeconomic development, on the other hand, point to its many failures: the marginalisation, social division and conflict it creates, and the competition it fuels. Both are probably partially right. Particular stages of the development process do generate conflict, and it is important for the development practitioner to recognise that conflict is an inherent part of development (both so that she or he is able to work with it, and in order not to deny its existence or its usefulness). Differentiation and organ (or sub-system) formation implies division. Eventually it is hoped that a healthy development process will lead to integration, but the passage through division, and often resultant conflict, cannot be avoided. It is a necessary component of the development process, a spur to further development, and there are times when it must be encouraged. In the example given above, had I, as a development consultant, been called in earlier I would have been faced with the task of facilitating the organisation through differentiation, through the creation of divisions and specialised sub-systems, rather than through integration. This might have resulted in a healthier development process had it been facilitated, but the phase of differentiation could not have been avoided. The development process goes through phases of separation as much as it does cohesion, and attempts to avoid division and conflict are often detrimental to the development process.

I shall return to considerations of the divisive elements of development when I consider development in the social realm. For the moment I would like to raise some other observations with respect to the issues that have been dealt with here. For any entity, phases of differentiation and integration do not occur as one-off processes. They recur and repeat themselves as the development process progresses. A phase of integration does not mean that differentiation will not recur; on the contrary, it is essential that differentiation does recur (as well as integration) on an ongoing basis, for, in the realm of human and social development at least, development does not have an end-point – we are always in a state of becoming. Indeed, to be able to recognise the human being as always in a state of becoming is an essential component of the respect with which the development practitioner needs to function.

In addition, pain is an integral part of development and cannot be avoided. It is not only, as we have seen, the spur to further development. It is also often the consequence of a particular developmental phase in the service of future development. This is not said to idealise pain, but rather to emphasise that its occurrence should not be denied or repressed.

Finally, as with human beings, the observation of how organisations develop reveals three further essentials. First, development implies new challenges, new responsibilities, and fundamental shifts in attitude and behaviour. Second, development is never 'instead of' but rather 'as well as'. In the example given, the developmental phase of integration, of incorporating reductions in conflict and tension, did not imply doing away with departments; rather than developing formal structures and procedures instead of specialised departments, the latter were retained as well as adding the coordinating structures. (Previous phases of development are incorporated in later phases.) Third, development is discontinuous. In the organisation mentioned, differentiation did not lead smoothly, logically and sequentially to integration. The organisation remained at the level of (unconscious and unplanned) differentiation for some years, until growth generated a crisis which led to a further development phase.

Summary

- Development is not growth. While growth entails a quantitative increase, and may precipitate development, development implies a qualitative change in structure.
- Development is a process in time, is discontinuous, and is mostly irreversible.
- Development moves through differentiation and hierarchisation to integration, in recurring cycles.
- Often a crisis is necessary to precipitate development; development is often accompanied by pain; development entails the need to let go of the past, to overcome resistance to change.
- Development is never 'instead of' but always 'as well as'.
- Development entails new challenges, responsibilities and shifts in attitude.
- Development entails division, and often conflict, moving through to integration, in recurring cycles.
- Development involves making current unconscious habitual patterns conscious in order to let go of them and to consciously embrace the new, unknown, phase. It requires a shaking off of routine, of stagnation. It is challenging, perhaps the greatest challenge we face. It is not only rewarding, leading to greater freedom, it is also necessary.

Interlude: Cohesion and Division

It was late at night. Outside the stars hung close and comforting, while inside the sparse fire burned brightly and through an open window drifted the stilling murmur of the Tra-Tra River as it flowed through the village. Wupperthal was asleep, yet we remained awake – they keeping the fire alive while I pushed at their thoughts in order to gain some understanding and clarity: an old man and an old woman, who had seen an eternity of such nights; and a young city-bred development worker, fighting himself.

I had been seduced by this community which seemed sufficient unto itself, which apparently had no need of me and had no impulse towards development. Yet everywhere I turned I found evidence of discontent, and so was forced to confront the paradox of an apparently contented community which was at the same time unhappy and discontented. On one level the community was socially cohesive; yet on the other it was shot through with division and conflict, with antagonism and tension.

In answer to my questions the old man put some more wood on the fire, slowly and thoughtfully. He did not speak. Yet tacitly he communicated with her, and she spoke from her place in the shadows.

'In the old days we cared for each other, and each of us was cared for in our times of need. We respected each other.' She stared into the fire. 'If we arrived at someone's house, we were fed and sheltered. Although our hosts might have had nothing, they would give us everything, because the Lord would provide the following day, or the Lord would not. We had nothing, we were dependent on His grace. All of us. Under such circumstances, how could we not give everything?'

No longer staring into the fire, she was looking at me and her eyes were lit by distress, indignation and anger.

'But it is all so different now. Sons and daughters have gone to the city to become nurses and teachers. They send back money to their families, some more, some less. Now some here build bigger houses, buy cars, buy generators and install TVs. Others have less money; many have none. Suddenly, people have, where before they did not have. And now there is selfishness. People hold on to what they have. There is pride and arrogance. We who have nothing are

17

looked down upon and scorned. We are no longer one. We no longer thank the Lord. We respect those who have, and what is this but disrespect for those who do not have?'

She subsided into silence and we each sat with our difficult and weighty thoughts. As the fire died down the embers glowed fitfully. I wrestled with myself, with my task here. Would development not worsen this picture and increase division? Development seemed to imply moving beyond dependence, becoming self-reliant and independent, and thereby separate. Was this not a cause of problem, rather than a solution? Yet it was happening anyway. How could a developmental intervention assist? The ambiguities of development were fragmenting my thoughts and forcing my mind into an ignoble retreat. I struggled to understand where the community was heading, and why.

2

Paths and Destinations

Phases of Development: Some Initial Thoughts on Direction

When you get to the top of the mountain, keep climbing.

Ancient Zen saying

Continuing the exploration into the essential nature of development, I would like to journey to another vantage point in order to gain a slightly different perspective on the development process. By looking at development from a fresh angle, I hope to deepen our understanding of the concepts with which we have been concerned, and to expand upon them. To this end we will explore the development phases of individuals and organisations.

What can be observed about the phases through which an individual appears to move on the journey through life? Are there indeed such phases and what are they; what can they tell us about the development process? I would like here to delineate three phases only. I believe these are the most easy to understand, the most uncontentious, the most apparent to the observer, and the most illustrative of the development process in its broadest sense.

People, as they move through life, move from the phase of dependence, through independence to interdependence. These, I would propose, are the three most basic and important phases of development. The childhood phase is the phase of dependence. The child is dependent on its parents and on social infrastructure for all of the elements of life: food, shelter, security, acknowledgement, and for socialisation into a particular culture. The phase of adolescence and young adulthood is a phase of increasing independence. The individual reacts to the dependence phase by asserting his or her independence; by breaking free of parental and social norms; by asserting his or her individuality; by revolt and resistance. All of us who are parents or who have been around young adults will attest to this observation. The independent phase is characterised by critique and rejection of the given norms; by developing individual identity through bouncing up against the world and defining 'self' through differentiating from 'the other'; by developing the ability and the inclination to say 'no'. When we can be critical, when we can question, when we are empowered to choose, when we can resist, then we have our independence and our individual identity.

Beyond this stage lies adulthood and maturity: interdependence. When we no longer have to assert our individuality and independence against the world because we are secure in ourselves we can achieve the recognition of ourselves as separate, coupled simultaneously with the recognition of our inevitable dependence on others. This, after all, is reality; we are, in fact, dependent on others in so many ways even while being independent individuals. But it is this very wisdom which, if it is lived more than on a merely intellectual level, allows us to grasp the stuff that life is made of honestly and effectively. Maturity and interdependence is the celebration of freedom within the bounds of real constraint. The ability to stand on our own in the midst of our dependence on others is always a challenge. It demands give and take. It demands tolerance and compromise. It is characterised by uncertainty, ambiguity and doubt. It demands an ability to see the other's point of view, and to recognise that there is more than one answer – one perspective – to an issue. Interdependence is not a state which is easy to maintain. We regularly slip back into the other two phases; indeed, many of us attain interdependence in but few aspects of our lives, and few achieve it in most.

These three developmental phases partake of the elements of development mentioned in the previous discussion. They take place over time, are often precipitated by crisis and pain, imply qualitative change, are discontinuous, and entail the need to let go of past phases, or to overcome resistance to change. They generate new challenges, responsibilities and shifts in attitude. They involve making current unconscious habitual patterns conscious in order to let go and to consciously embrace the new.

They also illustrate the point that subsequent development phases incorporate previous ones rather than rejecting them. Interdependence cannot be achieved without moving through, and retaining – albeit in a transformed state – the phases of dependence and independence.

Most of all they illustrate the move through differentiation, characterised by division and conflict, to integration, characterised by a 're-harmonising' of the whole. Dependence implies a certain homogeneity and 'oneness'; independence a certain separation and differentiation; and interdependence a conscious integration. This last point is vital because the phases of an individual's life are not described here in order to portray that life, but rather to illuminate the process of development itself. They occur wherever development is taking place, and they continually recur in an individual's life. We move from integration back to dependence, and from dependence to differentiation. We can never maintain a state of interdependence; we move back to dependence, reassert our independence, achieve interdependence once more. And while we may have attained a particular phase of development in one sphere of life we are at different phases in others.

For example, do not all marriages or partnerships go through various developmental crises on their journey through time which can be understood in terms of the concepts raised above? Where one partner is more independent than the other, the partnership consists only of dependence and independence and therefore maintains a level of separation, differentiation, and even conflict. It often takes the (successful) struggles for independence on the part of the dependent partner to force the crisis for the one who is more independent. This crisis can result in recognition of both partners' need for independence coupled with the embracing of the very real fact of their dependence on each other. A state of interdependence. Yet how difficult to maintain, either within our relationships or within our individual lives.

The scenario is a complex one, yet these similar patterns seem to repeat themselves continuously. In particular one factor seems to recur: life keeps distributing obstacles in our path, keeps returning us from interdependence to dependence, to maintain – or at least provide the opportunity for – the developmental impulse.

Why? It is not the individual life we are concerned with here, it is the developmental process itself. Where is it going? What are we developing towards? In Paulo Freire's terms, development occurs when one moves from dependence to a critical consciousness; the ability to analyse circumstance, to question existing reality, and to say no.[1] This, however, only corresponds to the stage of independence. I am saying that this is only partial development, and that interdependence is a phase beyond.

It is within this latter phase that the true impulse of development is illuminated. But in order to facilitate our further exploration of interdependence, let us first look at the foregoing dynamics from an organisational perspective. Typically, the developing organisation also moves through the phases of dependence, independence and interdependence.

The phase of dependence is that of the young, newly-formed organisation, led by one or more charismatic leader. The organisation is run almost as a family unit, personally and informally. Staff are generally content to follow the leader and are thus dependent on him/her. This does not initially or necessarily imply discontent. On the contrary, the leader is held in respect and regarded with esteem, and it is considered an honour to serve him or her (or them). The leader is personally involved in every aspect of the organisation, and in the private lives of the employees.

But this 'pioneer' phase – the phase of dependency – eventually becomes overripe, and crisis leads to further development. The crisis is generated by a number of possibilities and combinations of these. For example, the pioneer retires, dies, or simply cannot cope any longer with the expanding and growing organisation. Areas of organisational life become specialised, and employees begin to achieve a greater knowledge and competence in certain spheres than the pioneer. As the organisation grows the need for structures and procedures gradually eclipses informality. Staff are no longer content simply to follow – they have themselves been developing all the time. Alternatively those staff who no longer accept dependence leave, and the organisation is stuck with followers and loses its cutting edge.

At this point the organisation enters the phase of differentiation: the formation of specialised sub-systems, of formal structures and procedures. This is often accompanied by the loss of warmth, intimacy and the personal touch; it becomes more impersonal and objective, and it gains efficiency through division of labour, specialisation and standardisation. The individual staff member achieves independence: he or she is valued for a specific contribution, and outside of this lives his or her own life independent of the work sphere. Formal structures entrench impersonal independence; no longer dependent on a personal relationship with the pioneer, the employee is 'free' to provide a part of her life only, to sell his labour while maintaining independence in the personal sphere. Standardisation of structure and procedure ensures independence (for example, the impersonal equality and objectivity of salary structures and conditions of service).

The crisis of this phase enters when standardisation leads to feelings of isolation and alienation. Division of labour leads to loss of meaning, loss of creativity and lack of flexibility. Structures and procedures rule, and departments and individuals become separate, autonomous and no longer connected to, or contributing towards, the direction of the whole.

At this point integration is necessary. Attempts must be made to develop a more conscious organisation once again, one which is no longer driven by structures and procedures but by purpose, a sense of meaning and direction. It becomes necessary to form a team, to regain personal involvement and commitment, and to rekindle enthusiasm and creativity. We must look to the development of all staff as whole people, no longer as functional entities merely performing specific tasks. Leadership must be developed throughout the organisation. But most of all the organisation must become *conscious*. It has fallen asleep through specialised, repetitive activities and structured routines. In order to regain its cutting edge in the world it needs to become flexible and creative, responsive to the outside context rather than the internal routine.

Of course for an organisation steeped in procedure the reintroduction of individual flexibility and creativity, and of shared and revolving leadership, is difficult. It requires an entirely new attitude, coupled with trust in people rather than in systems. It is the developmental challenge of the integrated phase, when our developed sense of independence (our impersonal separation through structure and procedure) must be coupled with our dependence on people and our need to work together in a team.

Once again, organisational development displays the same elements of the development process as mentioned earlier with reference to individual development. Amongst others, these include the fact that these phases recur in organisational life: the phase of integration is difficult, if not impossible, to maintain; previous phases are incorporated in later ones and phases cannot be skipped. The integrated phase is not a reversion to the positive elements of the pioneer phase, thus rendering the intermediate, or differentiated, phase redundant. Rather, the pioneer phase was characterised by an unconscious, warm, simple and natural outpouring of activity and energy. Only by moving through independence – characterised by division, the coldness and contrivedness of structures and procedures, the isolation of individuality – is it possible to arrive at a point of interdependence, which is primarily a *conscious* attempt at integration. This requires huge reserves of tolerance for ambiguity and uncertainty. It demands a striving for balance between dependence and independence, and needs an awareness of context and an enthusiasm for creativity. Indeed, it demands the development of conscious leadership by all involved.

The foregoing is a crude characterisation of the phases through which an organisation passes. Every particular organisation only partakes in these phases to a certain extent. Yet an understanding of, and appreciation for, these phases can help the development practitioner enormously. This is the reason why different organisations need different interventions at different times; why one solution may work for an organisation at a certain time of its life, but not at others. I have seen attempts to restructure organisations fail when what was needed was destructuring, because the organisation was moving from independence to interdependence. I have seen pioneer leaders struggling because they lost step with their organisation when it moved beyond the pioneer phase and they were unable to transform or to encourage the independence of both staff and organisation. I have seen the efforts of community development workers to set up cooperative ventures and organisations come to nothing when those who were working in them did not wish for the level of responsibility that goes with the interdependent nature of the cooperative as organisation. These workers were at a different phase of their own development process, and had said that all they wanted was a job, to work for someone else. But the phase that they were at was not 'read' right or accepted. I have seen organisations try to form umbrella bodies, networks or associations, only to fail because the organisations themselves were either too dependent – without a real will or direction of their own – or too newly independent to engage with the kind of interdependent processes which are called for by the highly developed form of organisational association. I believe we can use these observations concerning development phases to begin to 'read', with intelligence, some of the developmental situations we face, and thus employ interventions which are responsive and appropriate rather than imposed, presumed and standard.

With these thoughts as background we can return for a moment to Freire's contention that development is the move from dependence to critical consciousness (independence). I believe these observations take us beyond this phase, to the phase of interdependence and to what I am going to call 'organisational consciousness'. Organisational consciousness is the phase which I have characterised as 'maturity' in the individual. It is the ability to act decisively within the realm of uncertainty, to continually seek the balance between polarities.

Dependence and independence. Leading and following. Structure and fluidity. Responsiveness and proactivity. The list is endless. Essentially, organisational consciousness entails being awake in, and to, the moment; having the awareness and resources within oneself to meet new situations coming towards one with creativity and acuity. I shall return to considering organisational consciousness in more depth in the following chapters. I would like at this stage, against the background of our observations thus far, to provide some initial thoughts as to the direction of the development process.

Whether we talk of critical or organisational consciousness, we invariably refer to consciousness. We have said that life itself appears to be in the service of development. It appears to me that life itself, through the development process, is striving towards greater consciousness. Every aspect of the development process attests to this striving. The state of dependence is a state of unconscious acceptance and natural conformity. Division, separation, and the pain which accompanies it – the stage of independence – represents the beginning of individual awareness. It represents a casting out from the security and safety of the hearth; the start of the individual journey; the insecurity of independent adventure and exploration. It embodies the loss and the fear involved in letting go of the nurturing environment. It represents self-reliance, a necessary step on the path towards becoming a full human being capable of contributing towards ongoing evolution.

But in itself this is not enough. It is unreal, for one thing, for our dependence on others and on the world around us is a fact of life. More importantly, however, it is not enough because in itself it heralds another form of dependence. The mode of denial with which it is associated, the mode of critique which is inherent in defining oneself by rejecting that which one is *not,* generates a new type of dependency. It is reactive, dependent on its opposite for its own definition. It asserts itself *against* a given reality, rather than in and of itself. The divisive nature of this stage of development implies the taking of sides, the identification with one section of the division rather than the other, the building up of a new 'culture' in response to the one which has been rejected. Rather like the athletes in a tug-of-war, the one side will collapse and disintegrate if the other side suddenly stops pulling. I remember how, in my late teens and early twenties, I was violently vociferous about the fact that I would not cut my hair, no matter how long it grew. It was my symbol of resistance towards a culture which had forced me to submit to the indignity and callous indifference of the barber's shears with such monotonous frequency and regularity. I was blissfully unaware of the fact that I had joined a new culture, and had become dependent on being recognised and accepted by that culture. At the time that long hair eventually became acceptable, as some years later it did, I no longer understood the rationale with which I had justified disentangling my hair from my belt every morning.

The stage of independence is essential in awakening consciousness, but is not enough to maintain it. The phase of interdependence, though, is that phase when I am secure enough in myself to be able to recognise and accept my dependence; it is the phase when I can define myself in and of myself, and so remain open, alive, awake and objective towards the world around me, towards others, towards both sides of the coin. For the coin is the thing; one side only cannot be the coin. Consciousness implies objectivity; it implies the faculty of self-reflection. It is the realm of true freedom, devoid of prejudice. It is the realm of responsible freedom, where one's individuality is exercised such that one's actions do not prejudice or encroach upon the freedom of others. It is the realm, not of 'us' and 'them', but of 'we'.

Life is striving towards consciousness. Life is in the service of development, the force and the process by which consciousness is achieved, which is why the process is a recurring one. Because consciousness is ephemeral. It can barely be described. It is an elusive state, extremely vulnerable and sensitive, yet at the same time a force of such power that despite its insubstantiality the conscious human being will be recognised wherever he or she is. However, it is a brutally challenging state and one which is difficult, in fact well nigh impossible, to maintain. For just when we think we have achieved it we lose it. Or when we achieve it in one area of life, we still struggle for it in others. Both the individual and the organisation, when they have achieved a new level of development, tend to fall asleep in that level and become mindless in the face of new routines, new culture, and the new paradigm. Indeed, when the new-found consciousness becomes a new paradigm, immediately we lapse into unconscious dependence on that paradigm once again.

Which is why life keeps throwing obstacles in our path and continues to provide us with the necessary challenges. Each new level of development, each fresh foray into consciousness, releases a new dependency and state of unconscious habit. Yet 'failure is to form habits.' The trick is to stay awake. The development process is a driving force towards greater consciousness, towards greater freedom.

Summary

Individual and organisational development processes move through three phases. The dependence phase is followed by a breaking away from the given towards a state of independence. The divisiveness of independence is in turn superseded by the phase of interdependence: the inclusive framework of 'we' rather than 'us/them'. Interdependence is achieved when we no longer have to assert our individuality and independence against the world because we are secure in ourselves and can achieve the recognition of ourselves as separate coupled simultaneously with the recognition of our inevitable dependence on others. These phases, and the transitions between them, partake of the insights generated around the concept of development in the previous chapter. Most importantly, phases cannot be skipped.

The progression of these phases is not linear, but is rather of a cyclical nature. We can never maintain a state of inter-dependence; we move back to dependence, reassert our independence, achieve interdependence once more. Life itself keeps distributing obstacles in our path in order to maintain (or at least provide the opportunity for) the developmental impulse. There is no end point in development.

Why then development? Where is it leading? Each developmental phase is a way-station on the path towards consciousness. The consciousness which is manifested in the phase of interdependence can be regarded as maturity in the individual, or organisational consciousness in the mature organisation. It is the capacity to make decisions with maximum awareness. It is the ability to act decisively within the realm of uncertainty and contradiction; to seek continually to balance polarities.

Life itself, in distributing the obstacles which wake us out of our inevitable routines and habits and thereby fuel the development process, appears to be in the service of development. Life itself, through the development process, is striving towards greater consciousness. Consciousness implies objectivity and the faculty of self-reflection. It is the realm of true freedom, devoid of prejudice. It is the realm of responsible freedom; individuality coupled with respect, care and active membership of the collective. The process of development is the means towards increasing consciousness, thereby increasing humanness.

Interlude: Resistance and Awakening

Battered cardboard boxes filled with goods had been unloaded from the truck and were stacked on the ground to one side of the dusty village square. I sat on one of them, shifting my boots restlessly in the dust, speaking quietly with those who stood or sat near me. Our attention was focused on the far side of the square. There, three figures stood in heated exchange. The breeze rustled the leaves in the trees, birds balanced on fence-wire, and old shiny-smooth cedarwood benches slept their ageless sleep in the sun. But the atmosphere was tense. I was simultaneously exhilarated and disquieted. We all awaited the outcome of the intense deliberations taking place between the three before making the next move. Not knowing what the next move would be.

After months of struggling fruitlessly with a people's soul which was at once older than me while at the same time dormant in submissive quietude, a spark had been lit and the village was awake and cracking with energy. Since before my time the people had been resentful towards the village's only shop, the general dealer which was housed in a large building on the edge of the square. The 'owner' of the shop was not a member of the community, and had a contract with the church in terms of which he ran the shop for his own gain. The shop was the one enterprise which had not been placed under the rubric of 'community development'. People were angry, yet helpless, at the exorbitant prices he could charge because of his monopoly. The nearest town was over 80 kilometres away over mountain roads, and the church did not allow anyone else to run a shop. I had stirred a new form of resentment by questioning not the prices or the monopoly but the fact that profits were being channelled to one person, and out of the community. The profits could be used for the community itself – the need was self-evident. The church complained continuously of the amounts it pumped into the village; the people asserted that they gained nothing from the church.

Individual conversations led to group discussions which led to meetings. Petitions and delegations were sent to the church, but to no avail. I then suggested that people form a consumers' cooperative; buy in bulk once a week from the nearest town, generate competition, force the issue, boycott the shop. I assisted with the organisation of this, but soon Sophie, who was a vibrant and energetic woman, unemployed and skilled, took over the complex and time-consuming organisational details. As membership grew a sense of ownership and power developed; people became involved and committed voluntary workers. Their skills and capacity for organisation grew.

The shop owner fought our efforts every step of the way. He cut off people's credit if they bought anything through the cooperative (and the inability of the cooperative to offer credit was a major stumbling block to a community which relied on it). He tried to block the cooperative form hiring trucks to bring the goods through from outside the village. He enlisted the help of the municipal authorities in the nearest town to declare the cooperative unlawful on health grounds. When the people won this last battle by calling the bluff of the authorities through the freely given offices of a civil rights law firm in Cape Town, there was no stopping the boycott, or the exuberant growth of the cooperative.

The shop 'owner' turned to the church, which came out to arbitrate – or to exert their authority – for the tide was turning against their wishes. Now Sophie stood on the far side of the square, face to blazing face with the head of the church and the shop 'owner'. I was hoping that the church had no legal argument.

The threesome broke up and Sophie came striding back across the square, grinning broadly. We surrounded her as she came up to us, shouting our questions. She answered none of them; she simply berated us for standing around idly when there were boxes to unpack. Whereupon there was jubilation; people were proud of their elected representative and bursting with pride at themselves, at their victory.

Some way away, Johannes looked at the celebrations with a dark anguish in his eyes. A worker in the shoe factory, I knew him to be a concerned member of the community and wondered why he wasn't celebrating with the rest. I walked over to him. He moved uneasily in my presence.

'What's the problem, Johannes?'

'That!' He gestured vaguely at the crowd unpacking boxes.

'But we've won, Johannes. You've won!'

'You think so?' He looked up at me, shook his head, and explained, patiently, as to a child:

'For better or for worse, the shoe factory has always depended on free transport to and from Cape Town on the trucks of Mr B. (the shop owner). For supplies and for marketing. You know we cannot cover the costs of that transport, and anyway there isn't any alternative. You think your cooperative is going to give a damn about our survival at the shoe-factory?' He turned and walked away, heading for his vegetable garden.

His characterisation of the cooperative as 'your cooperative' stung me, but not so badly as the truth of his words. The village had won, and the village had lost. Yet the village had palpably come alive. It crackled with a sense of future.

3

Social Development as Growth and Revolution

The Current Impasse in Development

...both our current problem and our future project should be
an educational practice whose fundamental purpose it is to
expand what it is to be human and to contribute to the
establishment of a just and compassionate community within
which a project of possibility becomes the guiding principle
of social order.

Roger Simon *Empowerment as a Pedagogy of Possibility*

We come now to that sphere of activity which is the true canvas
for the work of the development practitioner: the realm of
social development. What can we learn from observing the
history of development in this broader sense, and can we
apply – as a means towards understanding our observations –
the insights we have gained through looking at the
development process as process?

The problem of socioeconomic underdevelopment has been
a major issue of practical concern since the Second World War.
In spite of the increasing importance of this issue, the work
done towards alleviating underdevelopment and the
concomitant upsurge in theorising about it, the issue has not
gone away or even diminished. Rather, its relevance has
increased dramatically. The dilemmas of development, the
increasing gap between so-called developed communities and
so-called underdeveloped communities, have been expanding
at an alarming rate. Underdevelopment has become a major
international concern, and its ramifications are worldwide.
Purportedly, it poses a threat to stability and peace; in reality,

the very least we can say is that it threatens not only the lives but the very humanity of many millions of people.

I talk of underdeveloped communities rather than underdeveloped nations. Simplistic debates concentrate on the discrepancies between nations, notably between those of the so-called developed North (and West) and those of the so-called underdeveloped South (and East). Yet the problem of development is clearly more complex. Divisions exist everywhere. There is, for example, the rural/urban divide: the extent of poverty and lack of choice in rural communities as against urban communities. There is the employed/ unemployed divide, within both rural and urban communities. There are the divides, within the urban setting, between the suburban 'haves' and the sprawling township – or inner city – 'have-nots', and even between inner cities, townships and peri-urban squatter camps. And clearly, while the discrepancies between North and South exaggerate these problems in the South, they exist too within Northern 'developed' countries, to an increasingly – and alarmingly – large degree.

Further, the complexity of development implies that while the major manifestation of underdevelopment is widespread poverty and material 'backwardness', it incorporates problems of freedom, justice, human rights, equity and the abuse of power, as well as problems relating to the erosion of culture. Moreover, there is the problem of 'overdevelopment' which impacts on the realities of underdevelopment.

In the beginning, development thinking and action was dominated by the fact that development was looked at mainly from an economic view point. The need for development was connected with economic growth; indeed, economic growth was going to solve the problem of underdevelopment (economic growth and development were seen as almost synonymous). Further, theorists had an overwhelming faith in the power of forms of 'social engineering'; therefore, reducing underdevelopment was seen as largely a technical and economic exercise.[1]

This approach to development is, in essence, what characterises the theoretical perspective on development known as 'modernisation theory'. Simply, this approach implies the following: humankind is on a progressive advance from 'traditional' society – characterised by dependency on particular social forms and cultures, as well as on the whims and dictates of nature – to 'modern' society, characterised by control over nature, by individual free choice, by independence (freedom from given social and natural reality). The means to achieving this modern society was by way of economic growth – which implied control over (and freedom from) natural constraints, as well as reduction of poverty and consequently increasing freedom of choice. Modern society was therefore an industrialised society emphasising both production and consumption; under capitalist market conditions economic growth was to be the 'engine' of development. The history of Western capitalist society was viewed as the recipe for development. In other words, what one needed to do was to analyse the conditions which precipitated economic growth in Western society and apply one's analysis to the engineering of economic growth in underdeveloped countries; the result of this growth would be development.[2]

Put another way, the more growth there is, the more development there will be – if not immediately then in the long run. The benefits of growth would automatically reach all levels of society, an idea which came to be known as the 'trickle-down' theory of economic growth. Through industrialisation and commercialisation, developing societies would move inexorably towards 'modernity', or development. Obviously, this economic growth implies radical changes to the existing structures, patterns and cultures of developing countries, not simply in terms of shifts from agriculture to industry, from rural to urban societies, from certain political ideals and forms of organisation to others, but also to the whole cultural matrix which imparts meaning and gives coherence to the lives of people.[3] Non-economic factors are not ignored but are taken as conditions for the underlying economic process. Development equals economic growth which equals social engineering. Apply the principles of Western economic growth to developing countries, and development will result.

Now, this 'growth-plus-trickle-down' approach used the maximum increase in gross national product (GNP) per capita as its measure of development. Raise the growth rate of GNP and you will achieve development. There is no doubt that during the 1950s and 1960s, much success was achieved in raising the growth rates of GNP. Yet despite this the problems of underdevelopment continue. High rates of unemployment persist in developing, and latterly even in the so-called developed, countries. Inequality between nations has increased, not decreased. Inequality within nations, between communities, has also increased dramatically. The poor are getting poorer, and divisions and conflict are increasing. Not even the economic aspects of development are being realised, far less the social hopes which many have pinned on the development project: freedom, equity, justice and human rights.[4]

During the latter half of the 1970s it was contended that the elimination of poverty and the achievement of greater equality should supplement, if not replace, the growth of GNP as the target of development. This has been termed the 'basic needs approach'. No longer expecting high growth rates to achieve the trickle-down effect, policies aimed directly at meeting the basic needs of poor people would ultimately result in growth. Yet neither has this yielded significant results. Streeton, one of the founders of the basic needs approach, asserts that this is largely due to the lack of political will within developing countries to actually implement such a form of redistribution.[5]

One way in which to begin to understand the failure of these approaches is to take our insights concerning the nature of the development process itself, and apply them here. First, development is not growth. Development implies structural change with respect to the whole system. The modernisation approach equates development unequivocally with growth in GNP; the status quo is to be maintained while growth leads to development. Moreover, development is seen as a continuous process; there is no sense of timing, of the recognition that a particular level of development will be maintained until a structural crisis leads to a sudden leap to a new level. Modernisation theory assumes that development moves along a smooth and continuous upward path; there need be no radical shifts, nothing which will rock the boat or disturb the status quo. Indeed, development (as modernisation) was seen by its proponents as the instrument with which to maintain the status quo and protect the interests of the developed nations. So long as a critical mass of people receive some of the supposed benefits of modernisation, they will remain content and acquiescent. Yet we have seen that certain stages of development do not maintain either peace or the status quo; on the contrary, they lead to division and conflict, to complexity and differentiation, to the need for radical structural change affecting the whole system (thus, by implication, the developed nations as well – a consideration which is denied or avoided by most modernisation theorists).

Mostly, modernisation theory does not recognise the reality of dependence as a developmental phase, or the need to move from dependence through to interdependence – in spite of the fact that it views 'traditional' societies as dependent, and 'modern' societies as leading to increasing independence. Dependence is, perhaps, an aspect of traditional society, but dependence does not mean a state of childishness, of youth; it does not imply that economically developed nations can look down on underdeveloped nations as their inferiors. (Developed nations and communities have been doing this for years; it is a major component of racism.) Rather, dependence is a phase of development that continually recurs, that is returned to time and time again, in order to continue the development process. Dependence can take many forms, and be affected by external factors. One aspect of dependence is a 'falling asleep' into unconscious patterns of behaviour; submission to a dominant culture. To a certain extent, in terms of their 'traditionality', developing nations have often exhibited this dependence, and it has constituted the internal resistance to development. As such, it has not been taken account of sufficiently by modernisation theorists. Development cannot be imposed, created or 'engineered', it can only be nurtured and facilitated.

But there are also external reasons for dependence. In this sense, modernisation theory has conveniently failed to recognise that the conditions which precipitated the economic growth of developed nations cannot be replicated by developing nations because the dependence of the latter on the former is one of those very conditions. Both politically and economically a web of dependence of developing nations on developed nations has spread worldwide. And if development implies a structural change to the whole system, the developed nations themselves must be affected. They must, in fact, develop, and so cannot then be so simply regarded as 'developed'. This was never part of the original conception, which implies the failure of the development project through continuous – and smooth – economic growth.

Robert Chambers makes a similar point when he writes of the interrelatedness of poverty.[6] Poverty is not simply a function of the poor, the powerless, the marginalised. It is as much, some would say more, a function of the rich, the powerful, the few in whose hands resources and decision-making concentrate themselves. And the dichotomy perpetuates itself, not least because, as much as power feeds on itself, poverty generates a culture of poverty, which emphasises dependence and therefore undermines development.

The belief that the process of development was a smooth transition through economic growth generated particular forms of the development practitioner. On the international and national levels, we saw the emergence of technicians, economists, advisors and 'experts'. On more local levels the philanthropic initiative prevailed: people and organisations dedicated to welfare provision and to providing goods and services to and for people. At their most advanced, development practitioners of this ilk involved themselves in the development of local self-reliance. Community development here implied that local communities were to become less dependent and more able to contribute towards their own prosperity. These approaches to the practice of social development remain dominant to this day, and we will later explore their appropriateness and relevance.

One important aspect of all of these 'development practitioners' was their supposedly apolitical bias. Growth (so-called development) had little to do with politics, power, and dependency relationships between developed and underdeveloped. Growth was to be smooth, non-confrontational and non-divisive. The problem of poverty was the problem of the poor, and it would be solved by helping the poor to help themselves. It had nothing to do with the power structures within which the poor found themselves to be marginalised.

Enter, then, a new form of development practitioner: the activist. The activist was no longer development practitioner as apolitical do-gooder. Rather, the activist as development practitioner – as distinct from the activist as purely political being concerned with challenging the status quo on the political level only – saw it as his or her task to awake the poor, the marginalised and the oppressed to the political structures and dispensations which contributed to their continuing poverty. Indeed, the poor were no longer simply the poor; they were poor precisely because they were marginalised and oppressed. The task of the development practitioner as activist was to conscientise the poor, to stimulate their capacity for critique of the existing social order which maintained their poverty (à la Freire quoted earlier). The objective was to raise the consciousness of the poor from dependency to a critical consciousness capable of analysing existing power relations, primarily on the local and national level, and capable of responding to these by mobilising forces for political, economic and social change. The poor themselves, and their culture of poverty – and often silence – were part of the problem in that they allowed themselves to be oppressed; their dependency allowed them to be coopted into the maintenance of an unjust dispensation. They needed to develop a critical consciousness in order to break out of their own lethargy, dependence and acceptance of the status quo. They needed to develop the capacity to resist, to say no. The other part of the problem, however, was the oppressive structures themselves. Radical restructuring would be necessary before the problem of under-development would be adequately addressed. The alternative to the fiasco of growth was revolution.

This approach to development is embodied in the political economy perspective. The political economy critique of modernisation theory emphasises that evidence about the third world gives little support for the view that the benefits of growth do also spread to the poor. It thus becomes a vital task to explain why the growth process, rather than alleviating poverty, in fact increases poverty for large, and increasing, sections of the population on the local, national and international scene.

There are many schools of thought within the political economy perspective. Most are derivatives and refinements of the two original strands, the Marxist and dependency theories.[7] There is no need to go into the details of these various positions here. Suffice to say that the political economy critique, while originating mainly within the Marxist paradigm, is no longer confined to Marxist (or even neo-Marxist) thinkers. It is taken for granted among a broad spectrum of theorists, and there are certain salient and congruent points which are sufficient for our purposes here.

Control of political structures and of economic surplus determines the nature of the development process in terms of what kind of development takes place and who benefits from it. The internal class structure of countries and communities is one key to understanding control. The unequal relationships between nations forms another key, in the sense that penetration of a poor country by foreign capital results in political, economic and social change in the interest, not of the country itself, but of the country from which the foreign capital comes. In other words, lack of progress and development does not derive primarily from poor country, or community, inadequacies, but from various forms of external domination and exploitation. Revolutionary change means radical restructuring; it means devolving greater control and power to the marginalised wherever they are found. Development in this sense means structural change which affects both rich and poor, powerful and powerless, current stakeholders and marginalised. (Peter Berger has identified two myths which underly the theories of modernisation and imperialism: the myth of growth and the myth of revolution.)[8]

I have witnessed this process taking place on national and international levels. I have also been actively involved, as development practitioner, in these processes at a community level. I have worked in both urban and rural communities, at regional and local level, as both the apolitical and the activist development practitioner. I have been witness, and party, to the failure of welfare and the limited, partial success of the development of local self-reliance. Both internal inertia and external power structures conspired to maintain dependence. The original shift from welfare to the development of self-reliance was contained in the Chinese proverb attributed to Confuscius: give a man fish, and you feed him for a day. Teach him to fish, and he can feed himself for a life time. But what if the man, or woman, has no right of access to the lake? As activist development practitioner, I have seen communities rise up against prevailing power structures. I have seen how this has generated real self-reliance, shaken people out of a culture of silence and dependency, and shifted the prevailing social, economic and political dispensations. I have been privileged to have been part of such a process on a national scale. I have seen too how this has generated further problems for the pursuit of development. But I'm jumping ahead now. Let us first look at the political economy approach to development – the development practitioner as facilitator of critical consciousness – in terms of the observations concerning the development process itself which we have thus far made.

Clearly, the approach outlined above marks the true beginning of the development process in that it signifies the jump from the dependent to the independent phase. It clearly recognises that the independent phase is a phase of differentiation and division, which often leads to conflict, and it does not shirk from this recognition. It recognises that development is discontinuous and that it does not move continuously on a smooth upward path, but rather moves stepwise from one level to the next. Development is a process in time, and natural rhythms need to be respected. For development is not growth. While growth may precipitate development, it implies quantitative increase, while development implies a qualitative change in structure.

The development practitioner must judge whether economic growth has evoked enough pain amongst those excluded from its benefits to entertain the possibility of facilitating the development process towards critical consciousness. For often a crisis is necessary to precipitate development; development is often accompanied by pain, and entails the need to let go of the past and to overcome resistance to change. Growth which does not benefit the poor and which in fact increases their marginalised status often generates the pain and the crisis necessary to move to the next phase, to shake off the culture of dependency and develop a critical consciousness which can resist the prevailing status quo. As political and economic dispensations shift, development takes place both in terms of external benefits – economic as well as judicial and cultural – and in terms of the internal drive to self-reliance and independence. My own experience has witnessed the development of individuals towards leadership and independence as critical consciousness has achieved success in struggle. Development entails new challenges, responsibilities, and shifts in attitude. These take place primarily on the individual level before being incorporated into the community.

However, we have seen, in preceding sections, that the phase of independence, and of differentiation is but a stage in the development process. In itself, it bears the seeds of a new dependency which in turn requires transformation. Critical consciousness, definition of 'self' in terms of negation of 'the other', generates new paradigms in which we fall asleep once more and in which new unconscious behavioral and attitudinal patterns prevail. Division and conflict are not ends in themselves but may become so.

The history of struggle against prevailing social orders has revealed this tendency, not only on international and national levels but within communities and within segments of communities. In the wake of the development of critical consciousness, of structural change and new political and economic dispensations, new elites are formed. As a result new power structures develop and new divisions are created. New stakeholders come into being, or are incorporated into existing power structures, and the numbers of marginalised often increase. Critical analysis metamorphoses into a new paradigm, which in turn becomes a new ideology, potentially as enslaving as previous beliefs. Unconscious submission to the new ideology often generates mistaken programmes which are masqueraded as solutions. But mistakes are often denied or explained away in terms of the new paradigm. Critique becomes belief, and new forms of unconscious dependency are released. The new challenges, responsibilities and shifts in attitude become the seeds of new norms, new habits, a new dominant culture. A one-sided way of looking at issues persists; there is only one solution to a given problem, and this is the solution embedded in the new ideology. Approaching issues from different perspectives and employing a healthy eclecticism in utilising helpful elements from different paradigms or theories (some of which may be precisely the ones to have been discredited in the process of structural change) in order to bring different view points to bear on a particular issue, is often regarded as a betrayal of the cause and of the struggle for newfound freedom. Compromise is dealt with uncompromisingly. Divisions remain. We are stuck in the paradigm of 'us and them'.

We see this in the wake of many revolutions and situations of great structural change and upheaval. We have seen it occur in many former colonial countries where the tenets of political economy have ridden the course and new regimes have arisen. I have experienced it at local level within marginalised communities: struggles between township dwellers and squatters, between newly formed rural elites and their less fortunate neighbours, between recently unionised labour – incorporated into new dispensations – and the unemployed. People who were once 'brothers-in-arms', but, through structural change, new divisions are created, new stakeholders, new ranks of marginalised, and new theories to support the new divisions. Precisely the same phenomenon occurs in the so-called developed countries where the inherent attitudes of 'us and them', of smug patrony and covert defensiveness, maintain the divisions which face us all. Dogmatic adherence to the one answer and unrelenting clinging to power marks the stage of development at which we, as a global community, appear to have arrived. The phase of independence. The dialectic of critical consciousness become polemic.

There is yet a further dimension to the problems thrown up by both political economy and modernisation theories. Approaches within the political economy perspective differ on most fundamental issues with modernisation theory, but on two central elements they agree. These are the strong economic component of development, and the fact that, however we may get there, development implies a progressive advance towards a more 'modern' society, characterised by control over nature, by independence and by rationality; by technological mastery and commercialisation, and by economic abundance. Yet these very factors have generated problems in their own right, which in turn have raised new questions about world development. Some of these issues relate, at present, more to the developed than to the developing nations, and as such are regarded as being the possible consequences of 'overdevelopment', a relatively new concept which would have been unthinkable until very recently. Others relate to developing nations, as they 'progress' towards economic prosperity. Either way, they have given rise to alternative perspectives on the issue of world development which are sometimes grouped together within a theory called the 'contramodernisation' approach.

In essence, these perspectives amount to the realisation that the process of economic development can release excesses which are difficult to contain and which therefore pose real threats. Generally speaking they read as follows:

- There is an increase in poverty for the masses of the third world, even as – or perhaps because – certain countries become economically more developed. And within national borders there is poverty, growing unemployment and marginalisation in the midst of plenty, which often leads to social upheaval and instability.

- There is a rampant disregard for the devastation of the environment within which we live, and on which we remain dependent. Development in the form of independence has released us from our obvious dependence and interconnectedness with the natural environment, and has led to callous abuse. Economic growth, which relies upon the rape and pillage of our environment, has devastating consequences for us all. Not only is the environment itself under threat, but continued (economic) growth as well. Either way, the lifestyles which have become synonymous with development are not sustainable, or even attainable for the majority. At the same time increasing industrialisation has lead to social fragmentation and resultant frustration, anger and lack of personal fulfilment and meaning. Everywhere explosive nationalism is leading to ever greater divisions, fuelled by the proliferation of freely available weaponry.

- There is a growing crisis of meaning. As the old, traditional cultures fade, as individual free choice becomes the paramount goal, and as technology frees us from previous constraints, alienation becomes a real and burning issue. In a large part of the world the crisis of development lies in alienation, whether in misery or in affluence, of the masses. Increasing freedom from constraint and the resulting increasing complexity leave many people 'homeless': without meaning, without recourse to traditional explanation, without security. Our previous insights concerning the development process reveal this to be an inevitability; the phase of independence and differentiation is a casting out from the security of the hearth. (This is not, however, an answer or a solution; it is rather an indication that a search for the next phase is being precipitated.) As Peter Berger puts it: 'Modernisation operates like a gigantic steel hammer, smashing both traditional institutions and traditional structures of meaning. It deprives the individual of the security which, however harsh they may have been, traditional institutions provided for him. It also tends to deprive him of the cosmological security provided by traditional religious world views. To be sure, it gives him new opportunities of choice – that is, of freedom – but this new freedom is purchased at a high price'.[9]

Are these problems really the consequences of overdevelopment? Our observations appear to imply that, while they are indeed problems which result from the development process, they do not imply development gone wrong or the final consequences of development overreaching itself. Rather, as with the former problems relating to divisive conflict and the generation of new power structures, they are an indication that the development process has reached the crisis point of the independence stage; the struggle for the next phase is being forced upon us.

Summary

Two theoretical angles have dominated most development thinking. The first falls within the framework of modernisation theory; development as economic growth. This stresses social engineering towards economic growth and the 'modern' society. It has proved largely unsuccessful, although still pursued, primarily because: firstly, it has assumed development as continuous economic growth, thereby misunderstanding the nature of development as discontinuous and demanding qualitative structural change to the whole system, which would include the developed nations themselves; secondly, it has avoided the contradiction of dependence, the fact that the 'developed' world creates the very conditions for maintaining the phase of dependency in the 'underdeveloped' world; thirdly, it does not understand the element of time with respect to development, and that development cannot be imposed. It has given rise to the apolitical development practitioner, by and large as unsuccessful as modernisation theory itself.

The framework of political economy generates a far more accurate and developmental paradigm. Essentially it asserts that control of political structures and economic surplus determines the nature of the development process in terms of what kind of development takes place and who benefits. The marginalised, dispossessed and oppressed are to be encouraged to rise up to independence, to change radically existing political, economic and social dispensations. Not just economic growth but structural change is needed. Enter the activist development practitioner. However, the danger of the political economy approach lies in the divisiveness and conflict which characterises the phase of independence. Polarised thinking necessary to the development of independence becomes entrenched. Critical analysis metamorphoses into a new paradigm, the new paradigm into a new ideology, and critique becomes belief. A new dependency is created, and a new 'us/them' dichotomy. This heralds the search for further development.

The similarities between modernisation and political economy theories speak to the same need. Both paradigms stress modernity and economic growth. In both developed and underdeveloped communities, the near exclusive emphasis on these two factors gives rise to increasing poverty and marginalisation, environmental rape, social fragmentation and violence, and a crisis of meaning.

The advent of contramodernisation perspectives heralds the search for new meaning with respect to the development process.

Interlude: Dialogue and Isolation

Prior to my arrival in Wupperthal the few small industries and the shop had been run by a white man, an immigrant from Europe whom the church had brought in 18 years before – ostensibly to run the economic affairs of the community on behalf of the church. In fact he had been given a monopoly over all financial activities, had run them for his own profit, and for these last 18 years had ruled the community in a dictatorial fashion. In addition to the store, the two factories and the tannery, he possessed most of the arable land, apart from the pieces which individuals were alloted for subsistence farming. Every way the community turned, there he was. And he used the community cruelly, denying wages, denying credit, denying work, denying basic rights, all at his own discretion and apparently in response to his mood of the moment.

Eventually the community got rid of him: they burned his house down. At that point the church recognised that the situation had got out of hand, and asked him to leave. He went to Cape Town with his wife and children, built himself a mansion in a plush suburb, and sent his children to university. The community was left as poor as it was when he arrived, but at least it was free.

There were celebrations, and much thumping of fists into palms as stories were told about how 'we' had done it in the end, and how we were taking charge ourselves now, and about time too, because he treated us like slaves. But now we'll be our own bosses, and did you see the way the house burned that night, and how the bliksem *had to flee with his family in the police van from the neighbouring town in their pajamas.*

I had arrived a few weeks before he finally left. This was to be a new era, said the church, and I was to help the community to develop itself. What the church seemed to mean by this was that I was the cheapest way of pushing the problem of the community onto a dusty shelf where it would safely lie ignored for the next few years and not bother them again. Or perhaps they were simply at a loss themselves as to how to care for economic issues. And the community was simply content that its oppressor had left.

But contentment doesn't last – not when your land is barren, your clothes are threadbare, your resources are thin and you feel abandoned. But abandoned by whom? Abandoned, in fact, by the

47

very man who had oppressed them for 18 years. The community wanted him back. They felt they could not do without him. Stories began to emerge of how much he'd done for them in spite of his cruelty, even by means of the cruelty itself. And they did not feel competent to carry on without him because no-one wanted to lead.

I didn't understand this at the time. I felt contentment gradually overtaken by despair, like sand slipping through the fingers and blown away on the wind. I was left wondering what was going on. Where was the people's pride, backbone, or whatever it is that keeps you standing when the wind howls and the dust rises and all that you want to do is screw your eyes shut and turn your back and huddle up under the donkey cart but instead you face into the wind and keep your eyes open and look for the path which will lead you through this skin-scraping grit-laden storm? I became angry, found others who were also angry, and organised a meeting in the communal hall; a meeting that was attended by many.

Nothing very structured happened that night. People were asked to reminisce in small groups and to examine their experience of the past 18 years. But they were asked especially to listen to others' stories rather than to concentrate on telling their own. For people had been talking and talking and talking in an extravagant barrage of words, and no-one had stopped to think, to listen, or to hear.

Nothing was written down, nothing was planned or resolved. People simply spoke, and were heard. And slowly it seemed as if a tentative understanding began to emerge. A very old man, spare and thin as the terrain in which he lived, rose to address the meeting. A grizzled man, grey and lined, whose eyes burned in his head as though they were consuming his old body in fire. A man whose voice rattled like a slide of rocks down the side of a dry hill.

'I have been alive a long time, and all that time the Bible has been my closest friend. But I never could understand, in all this time, the meaning of the story of the Israelites' exodus from Egypt. Why did they wander 40 years in the desert? Because no-one who had been born a slave in Egypt could enter the promised land. Why? Tonight, at last, I know why. Because when a people is pressed down, ground underfoot like a worm, when this happens for long enough, then the people begins to feel that it is a worm. And when the boots go away, and the worm can stand up once more, it is too late. The worm cannot stand up, because it no longer knows that it has feet. It believes it is nothing more than a worm.

'Our tragedy is not that that man was here, or that he did the things he did, or that he is no longer here. Our tragedy is that we believe we cannot do the things he did, that we need him. Our tragedy is that we believe what he wanted us to believe. We believe him, and not ourselves.'

He was not preaching to the community, he was an expression of the communal learning which had taken place that night. So there was a collective murmur of agreement when he said, 'But its not true. We can make a choice.' And the old man led all the people out of the hall into the stony gravel square before it, so that they could, as he said, look at the stars once more, and realise that they were free.

That gathering in the square became even more poignant for me a few days later when the shockwaves from a small item of news reverberated through the community. The European immigrant, in the basement of his new mansion in Cape Town, had committed suicide by shooting himself in the head. He had left a note for his wife expressing his loneliness and his feeling of abandonment.

By whom had he been abandoned, I wondered. He was worth over a million rand, earned through a community which had nothing. And then I realised that he had been as dependent on these people as they had been on him. He had needed his 'slaves' as much as his slaves needed him. Perhaps more so, because they at least had each other; he was alone. He was trapped in a nightmare, believing himself the master, yet held prisoner by this belief. Unable to be master any longer, he chose death over freedom.

The people had chosen differently. I could only conclude then, and still believe now, that the people's ability to enter into dialogue with each other, and through this dialogue to learn something about themselves, was the key to ridding themselves of an unhelpful paradigm. The master, on the other hand, had been isolated, unable to explore in dialogue with others, and had therefore failed to unravel the knot which he himself had tied. And the knot had swollen over the years so that in the end he had pulled at it with weak and wasted fingers in a futile attempt to loosen the strands. It needed more than him alone.[10]

4

Development as the Building of Civil Society

New Directions for Development

If we were to find a key to the explosive condition of the world it could only be done by holding contraries together. That was the key.

Lindsay Clarke *The Chymical Wedding*

We have learned that an impasse should not signal despair but rather the need for another leap forward, for a letting go of the old in order to embrace an unknown future. In letting go we will perhaps discern an intimation of that future. Clearly we have reached an impasse with respect to social development.

Modernisation theory, with its singular emphasis on growth and linear, continuous progression which assumes no change in the status quo, cannot answer the requisites of the development process. On the other hand, the political economy perspective marks the beginning of that process, with its focus on independence, conflict and differentiation, radical structural change and social renewal. The impasse, however, in which the 'myth of revolution' leaves us is typical of the phase of independence – differentiation and division become entrenched in ongoing conflict, fragmentation and rigid new paradigms. And the myths of both growth and revolution leave cultural and meaning vacuums in their wake, leading to alienation and the erosion of common, traditional value systems.

In South Africa, for example, these processes have been sharply illuminated because a society which has undergone a radical transformation to a new political dispensation is also a society characterised by vast tracts of traditional culture which have been shaken through the demands of both economic growth and political transformation. An illustrative example concerns the youth of the country. An educational system which was both symbol and perpetuator of white hegemony became a site of struggle for black youth, who rallied under the banner of 'Liberation before Education'. Their power was a major factor in precipitating transformation, yet in the process a 'culture of struggle' was born, and this new paradigm carried forward into the transformed South Africa. A generation of South African youth are now known as 'the lost generation', not least because they are battling to transform their hard won 'culture of resistance' – which has succeeded in gaining so much – into a 'culture of education'.

Moreover, traditional society in South Africa places a high value on respect for elders. In the process of battling the apartheid regime, youth battled their parents as well because they were viewed as tolerating an unacceptable status quo. In the wake of transformation, the traditional relationships and sources of meaning between the generations have broken down, and the result is a new generation of township youth, many of whom reject parental authority, regard the streets as their home and armed gangs as their family. Breakdown in tradition and culture has economic roots as well. Economic 'progress' has meant the erosion of rural subsistence livelihoods, the cities are becoming inundated and untenable with unemployed and 'unskilled' (in the industrial sense) workseekers, and the problems of alienated youth have increased exponentially.

These pictures are repeated in many areas of South African society. Traditional tribal authorities who joined with more 'secular' parties in the struggle against apartheid were set adrift when the new democratic nation inevitably called the old traditional forms of tribal authority into question. Many people have been left stranded, caught between worlds where traditional authority and gender roles are no longer acceptable in the new dispensation. And many of those who have fought long and hard for this new dispensation have had to drink deep of the waters of resistance and conflict, and in the process of attaining their long-sought independence have found it difficult in the extreme to engage with processes of negotiation and reconstruction which demand a culture of give and take, of interdependence. Thus, for instance, rent boycotts which successfully crippled the apartheid regime are often still enforced against a new democratic government striving for reconstruction. Generally a culture of resistance still dominates where the demands of reconstruction are clear to all.

Success, then, has created new problems. Not surprisingly, given our previous analysis. The successful adoption of independence has awakened and empowered through a process of division, separation and conflict. But new and untenable mores and approaches have become entrenched in the process. A further step is needed. Nothing has been done incorrectly; it is simply that independence is only one phase in the process of development. What then is the next step? What is meant by the phase of interdependence when applied to the social realm?

I would like to tackle this issue from two perspectives, which lead out of the two sets of difficulties outlined above. The first set concerns the consequences of the myth of revolution and refers to ongoing division, marginalisation, conflict, and the entrenchment of new ideologies, paradigms and power cliques. The second set emerges in the myth of growth, and particularly 'overdevelopment'. It encompasses the issues faced by progressive modernisation: the erosion of meaning and security through increasing rationality, secularisation and freedom of choice.

Both revolution and independence are inseparable from the concept of power. The struggle for independence is a struggle for power; a struggle to replace the power of others with one's own power; a struggle for the resources which are controlled by power; and a struggle for the power to identify oneself in one's own terms rather than in terms defined by others. This struggle leads to critical consciousness, to awakening and to action, and constitutes real development. Glyn Roberts' definition of development therefore strikes a chord in the hearts of activist development practitioners: 'Development is the more equal distribution of power among people.'[1] He contends that power is the lowest common denominator of development; without shifts in the balance of power, development cannot be said to be taking place. This realisation, this definition, is, as we have seen, a vital developmental step. Without it, we are really only playing games when we talk of development. Time and again, between nations, within communities, within organisations, I have seen development taking place only when the powerless become empowered in the face of the powerful. But it is, as we have seen, only a stage in the process, and in itself can lead to the kinds of problems mentioned above. While it is a necessary condition for development, it is not sufficient. Getting stuck in the phase of independence leaves us stuck within a particular concept of power: power 'over', or 'against', others. We need to move beyond this.

Roberts, in his definition of development as the more equal distribution of power, refers to three different types of power: political power, economic power, and cultural power, or hegemony. Although different, all of these incorporate the same concept of power, that is, power over others and the capacity to coerce others to do one's will. As such, while demanding redress by those over whom power is exerted, they release in those struggling through dependence towards independence the very attitudes which characterise those who hold 'independent' power over others – attitudes of 'us and them', of uncompromising division and conflict, of definition of self in terms of negation of others, superiority and the need for coercion.

Thus development in the independent phase demands the more equal distribution of power but does little to diminish the negative consequences of power as the capacity to coerce others. Divisions and power blocks remain, although the dominant players may change; indeed, even while the players are developing, this definition of development allows the development process to move only so far, and no further. The struggle for independence may lead to empowerment – the ultimate cliché of the development fraternity – but leaves the one thus empowered with the same kind of power as those who had been fought against precisely because they had this power.

Is there another concept of power towards which we could strive as a way out of the dilemma? Power more characteristic of interdependence than independence?

In approximately 150BC the Jewish people were colonised and oppressed in their homeland, in what was the equivalent of modern day Israel, by the Greeks. The Greeks were far more cruel as invaders than were the Romans who came later; they were intent on wiping Judaism off the face of the earth, and thus attacked not merely the land and the people but particularly the Jewish culture and religion. At the time there lived a family of five brothers, who became known as the Maccabees. The Maccabees led the revolt against the Greeks – the struggle for liberation and independence – and became a source of pride and legend. When they began the revolt, knowing that they had killed and would inevitably kill many times more before liberation had been won, they had to overcome a basic precept of their religion, namely the injunction against the taking of life. 'Thou shalt not kill', was the commandment. Yet, 'Thou shalt have no other gods before me' was another, and the Greeks were forcing them to forego their religion in this sense. One way or the other they had to transgress. They chose war.

Being forced to choose in this way did not free them from the knowledge of transgression; they could not use it as an excuse. They felt that by taking the path of war, by killing, they were forfeiting their right to lead their people when the war would be won. For, although they had been forced into this, they would no longer be fit to lead. They would be tainted in some profound way and would have lost their truth. Yet there was no other way. So they did an interesting thing. One of the brothers was asked to swear that he would not enter the war and that he would not kill, in spite of how this might have seemed to others (and to himself). This brother was to remain free, pure, and therefore fit to rule. He became known as the lawgiver, and did in fact fulfil the future which had been ordained for him when the other brothers were rendered unfit to rule through their 'misuse' of power.[2]

There is a profound truth which underlies this legend: a recognition that the struggle for independence, that power taken in this way, becomes rigid through the manner of its taking, and tainted through its conjunction with the opposing power that has been defeated. The struggle is necessary, as is independence and the power taken, but something else is needed to move us beyond the contradictions. A new and different form of power. The power of the lawgiver in our story. What is the nature of the power which is fit to discern reality and rule a nation?

Scott Peck provides us with an insight when he identifies a form of power other than political, economic or cultural power. He refers to this form of power as 'spiritual power'. 'Spiritual power ... resides entirely within the individual and has nothing to do with the capacity to coerce others ... It is the capacity to make decisions with maximum awareness. It is consciousness.'[3] Coming to power in this sense implies the struggle for greater consciousness in that we do not fall asleep into new paradigms or ideologies; on the contrary, we must recognise our own limitations and the constraints of our current knowledge. We need to develop the faculty of self-reflection, of humility in the face of the unpredictability and uncertainty of life. We must recognise that we are often most in the dark when we are most certain, and the most enlightened when we are the most confused. It implies that there are no easy answers, no quick fixes; that life is ambiguous at all times, that each move we make in our attempt to effect the appropriate solution to a problem releases new problems and new difficulties. We need to consider our options carefully and weigh the consequences. We need to compromise, to recognise that the lines between ideologies, paradigms and different camps are not necessarily as rigid and impermeable as they may first appear. When you are involved in revolution, in the struggle for independence, you cannot give in to these uncertainties, these questions, these doubts. Your task is to be strong and hard, sure and right. This is the way rebellions and independence are won, with quick answers, no compromise, and solutions which ignore the problems they raise. This is the way of independence. But the power that is interdependence is something other.

Put another way, development moves from independence to the phase of interdependence when, having gained the critical power of independence, we are 'empowered' enough, secure enough in ourselves, to transgress boundary lines, to recognise our limitations and constraints and the realities of our dependence on others, and to work beyond the attitude of 'us and them' into the attitude of 'we'. We are all in this thing called life together. There is no one ultimate theory, no ultimate paradigm, no ultimate ideology, no ultimately correct political party, clique or social movement. To move beyond the crisis generated by independence we need to relearn humility. Not the subservient humility of the phase of dependence, but the conscious humility of interdependence.

The process of development moves us from acceptance to critique, and then – when critique has generated a new mindset, a new hegemony or status quo – it can move us to a new level of awakeness, of consciousness, by insisting that honest self-reflection be used to break down newly formed boundaries and divisions in order that interdependence be recognised and struggled for.

From dependence, through differentiation and division, to integration, as we have previously observed. Both Scott Peck and Berger point the way to integration. Scott Peck talks of the need for self-reflection to achieve greater consciousness. Berger talks of the need for raising difficult questions in order to cross boundary lines between opposing models or encampments.[4] Here lies the key. Critical consciousness – the phase of independence – begins the development process by recognising the need for, and demanding, radical structural change. When we inevitably lapse into the unconscious acceptance of new divisions and paradigms, the work towards integration begins with the raising of questions. Raising questions is always a dangerous enterprise, particularly when one begins to question oneself, one's assumptions, one's (often unconscious) paradigms, and one's comrades. It is not the task of the phase of independence, when the task is to challenge and critique others. It can only be done when one has developed enough strength to be vulnerable; and yet it must be done in order to develop this strength, the strength of interdependence.

What do we mean by this capacity for self-reflection and self-questioning? Laurens van der Post, in his novel *A Far-off Place*, writes: 'and remember all men tend to become the thing they oppose. The greatest and most urgent problem of our time was to find a way of opposing evil without becoming another form of evil in the process. Hence the New Testament's enigmatic, "Resist not evil." ... One had to reject corruption by suffering as much as corruption by power, be equally uncompromising and unsentimental about both.'[5] There is no question but that one has to resist evil, to assert one's power and realise one's independence. Even by force if all else fails, for there are times when force must be met with force. But there is development beyond this point, as there is danger in getting stuck in the mode of resistance if one does not act from a centre of consciousness and awareness as protection against contamination. Here, self-reflection and self-questioning are both prerequisites as well as benchmarks.

I was once facilitating an organisational development process within a South African non-governmental organisation when a conflict between two individuals revealed itself as both a major stumbling block towards organisational resolution as well as the symbolic centre of all the tensions and polarities that were tearing the organisation apart. Both protagonists were men. The one was white, from a wealthy community, highly educated, born to power and to leadership, and a director of the organisation. The other was black, far less educated, from a working-class background, and a middle-level staff member. For more than a year most members of the organisation had been in conflict with the leadership, and had been at pains to explain what they felt was wrong about the leadership's conduct. But leadership, and particularly our protagonist here, would not listen. Perhaps he could not hear. He insisted that he was doing things right, and that people were misunderstanding his intentions and misinterpreting his actions. But during an organisational workshop the issue finally came to a head in front of the 30 people present.

There was silence in the room as David – for such we shall call the middle-level staff member – tried to explain himself for one last time. He talked of the differences in their backgrounds. He talked of how his best friends during his school days had been white, and of how when school was over they had studied further or obtained good jobs because they were socialised to expect this for themselves; whereas he, socialised differently, had gone to work packing shelves in a shop. He did not believe that any other future was open to him.

Now, he said, 'a few days ago, you, Peter' – as we shall call the white director – 'and I were walking along the road together, in town, when we realised that we had to make an important business call. You walked into the first office block you saw and asked the receptionist if you could use the 'phone! You clearly felt this was your right. Do you realise how this made me feel? Left on my own I would have walked across town looking for a public call phone which worked, because this is what I have been conditioned to regard as my place. Every time you act, without thinking, you undermine my quest for independence. Can you not look at the life you have been given? Can you not begin to see the dynamic here, even if it is unconscious and inevitable?'

The intensity and honesty of the group process at this point succeeded in shattering the boundaries which individuals had placed around themselves. This, coupled with the integrity and depth of despair which elicited David's outpouring, and his ability to allow himself to be vulnerable, enabled Peter to begin to understand, to 'see'. For the first time this man, who had lived a life of independence, was able to see himself. For the first time he was able to see the world surrounding him with an approximation towards some form of objectivity. And he was able to begin the shift towards a new developmental phase in his life, towards interdependence. And David, who had felt so dependent, who had been working towards independence for years, had eventually achieved it and taken the courage in hand to go beyond it, to risk himself, to open up his vulnerable core. Two protagonists immersed in their need for independence were able to move beyond and resolve conflict without loss of face. And not only they but the entire organisation was enabled to move into a new developmental phase, a phase which incorporated both dependence and independence, and transformed them. And interestingly the sum of power in the organisation was increased, and no-one's power was decreased.

Self-reflection and questioning leads to a new kind of power: the power of consciousness and of the capacity to make decisions with maximum awareness. Thus with an attempt at objectivity, at what Buddhism calls disinterest or non-attachment. The ability to see both sides, to transgress boundaries. Perhaps we could say simply that the phase of inter-dependence entails the power to see, and to act on what we see. The poet Rilke exposes the heart of the issue when he writes 'take your well-disciplined strengths and stretch them between two opposing poles. Because inside human beings is where God learns.'[6]

What does all this mean for social development? How do we move beyond the necessary but divisive stage of independence which we have reached, and which has brought us to a developmental impasse?

Taking our cue from the foregoing, we need to envisage a society capable of self-reflection, capable of questioning its own paradigms and assumptions. A society which has not fallen asleep into cliques and power blocks but which is awake, self-critical, and searching rather than presumptuous. A society which curtails the excesses of power, which is able to hold itself open. A society which rigorously tests its fundamental premises rather than elevating them into fundamental and supposedly self-evident truths. A society which has moved beyond conflictual schisms into a phase of negotiation and compromise. A phase of maturity as a move towards greater development. A phase of interdependence.

It seems to me that the only way to mediate such a situation, once a significant level of independence has been attained, is through the promotion and facilitation of a strong civil society, one which can curb the hegemonic forces contained in the various power spots which accumulate and grow. The image of a strongly developed civil society is one in which the power of the state, of capital and of transnational capital and transnational 'aid' organisations, is held in balance by a plethora of competent, independent and self-reflective community-based and non-governmental organisations. One in which, according to Narsoo, 'there are a thousand buds of power blooming, where there is a rich texture and depth of organisation, and where debate, creativity, innovations and self-expression abound...'[7] As Narsoo notes, the concept of civil society is a contested terrain, insofar as the exact extent and limit of state intervention versus the integrity of civil society activity remains an open question. I do not wish to engage in this debate here. Indeed, I do not believe there can or should be a hard and fast answer – it is precisely the point that the balance between the organs of state, capital, international interests and civil society remains in a state of flux, capable of adaptation and improvisation in response to particular circumstances.

My contention that development – that interdependence – involves the building of civil society arises from the fact that, without such a social component, debate itself is impossible. Where either one of state, capital, foreign government, international commerce or civil society dominate, a hegemony of interests arises, and we, once again, fall asleep into specific dominant paradigms. The emergence of a strong civil society will necessarily be a complex and confusing process, giving rise to new problems, new uncertainties and ambiguities. Experience in South Africa, for instance, has demonstrated that the clarity and partnership between the forces of change before the transition necessarily gave rise to a confusing, and partially debilitating, struggle to understand the new roles of both government and civil society once independence had been won. As we have seen, this is essential for development. The more debate, the more possibility of multifarious perspectives. Development and evolution, as we saw earlier, tend towards complexity; also towards organisation and consciousness.

The fundamental issue for a developing society (and all societies are developing), the essence of the search for the next phase of development, for a way out of the current impasse, is consciousness. If consciousness is the ability to stay awake and aware, to hold opposites in balance, to achieve self-reflective objectivity and flexibility, to increase the sum of power without diminishing people's independence, then the extent of a society's consciousness – read 'development' – will be measured by the strength of its civil society. Only a multitude of freely operating, competent people's organisations will ensure that the dangers of hegemony, fundamentalism and dogma are reduced. Both the monopoly of interests potentially in the hands of the state, as well as those exercised by monopoly capitalism, will only be challenged by a vibrant civil society. If we are serious about 'people-centred development', a development approach which genuinely works from the bottom up, which ensures that people themselves are not only at the centre of development efforts but are also to be encouraged to take responsibility for their own development, then the facilitation of the building of the institutions of civil society becomes the true realm of the development practitioner.

If we further wish to ensure sustainable development, environmentally sound and socially just production processes, then, more than ever, we cannot leave the fate of a nation or of a community in the hands of the few. Responsible freedom and productivity need to be placed firmly in the hands of the many. A society with a developed civil component is one in which 'more people have access to resources and power over choices'.[8] A conscious society.

We have looked at the fact that while the independent phase is the phase of critical consciousness, the phase of interdependence is the phase of organisational consciousness. For the individual, there is no greater learning ground for interdependence than the contradictions and uncertainties inherent in organisational life. The individual who can perform competently within a developing organisation, an organisation which has itself reached the phase of interdependence, is an individual who has developed maturity in the sense of organisational consciousness. (The contradictions inherent in organisations, and the alternating states of dependence and independence inherent in the fluctuating dynamics of group life, require a mature integrity and flexibility for their successful negotiation.) The phase of interdependence can be attained through the growth of the organisational capacity of individuals and communities themselves. This growth in organisational capacity and organisational consciousness is the key to unlocking the next phase of development. The radical structural change needed now is the growth of organisational consciousness through the proliferation of people's organisations.

The second set of issues outlined above as the inevitable consequence of the independence phase of development – labelled overdevelopment – points, for their resolution, in the same direction. Progressive modernity and economic growth, underpinned by rationality, secularisation and freedom of choice, create a crisis of meaning. Where people previously lived in unified, relatively simple social structures, they now come to live in structures that are enormously variegated, organised in extremely complex ways. This has profound implications in all institutional areas, from the integrity of religion or culture to the stability of family relations. Alienation, lack of connectedness and of a sense of belonging, result in individual anomie, in social upheaval, in environmental rape. New approaches are needed to achieve integration within continuing differentiation and the inevitable pluralism of modernity. People themselves need to begin to put their lives together once more, to create collective meaning, to find together new (freely chosen) guiding principles. These are no longer given; we can take nothing for granted. But the homeless need to build new homes; wanderers need codes of conduct for the road. These will differ from community to community, from nation to nation. But genuine idealism and enthusiasm and respect, so essential to human endeavour, must be rekindled – or else we face continuing disintegration and fragmentation.

Here, Berger points out, 'The paramount task ... is the quest for intermediate structures as solutions to this dilemma of modern society – structures which will be intermediate between the atomised individual and the order of the state. American pluralism, even in its failures, provides a unique object lesson to anyone concerned with this problem. Conversely, the variety of institutional experiments and compromises now going on in the Third World offer highly suggestive lessons towards the same end.'[9] This implies, once again, the devolution of power to civil institutions capable of contextual analysis and conscious compromise and experimentation. Civil institutions which can curb the abuses of power and create meaning by, and on behalf of, their members. People's movements which can negotiate, seek alternatives and compromises. People's organisations which can produce, and create prosperity, by and on behalf of their members.

Civil society in the form of a multitude of vibrant and variegated organisations can continue the process of development towards integration, towards a more conscious society and a more conscious individual, capable of redressing division and imbalance, experimenting with new forms of meaning, creating new productive structures and possibilities. The emergence of a strong civil society counteracts the various forms of marginalisation inherent in the phase of independence. This is 'people-centred development', as opposed to the provision of services or the struggle for power.

Naturally, civil society is no panacea. There is no ultimate truth. It is not 'the answer', and, in any event, development – as we have seen – is a recurring process. There is no end point. But the struggle for civil society is the struggle towards a more conscious, a more wide-awake society capable of self-analysis and self-reflection and the righting of imbalances as they occur – as they inevitably will as new routines, habits and preferences reassert their unconscious force. The concept of organisational consciousness is a humanising picture of development; development in the service of consciousness as the unfolding of human potential. In *Beyond the Impasse – New Directions in Development Theory*, Frans Schuurman seems to end the book's deliberations with similar thoughts. He notes that 'Writers like Foucault and Deleuze ... pointed out the existence of multiple discourses within society which act as counterpoints to the hegemonic power ideology which tries to colonise the inner life-world.'[10] He then goes on later to say that 'To overcome the disjunctive discourses it is vital to view these (social) movements in terms of an emancipatory force trying to enter into the aborted modernity project in underdeveloped countries.'[11]

Here, the development practitioner is no longer activist, no longer someone who takes it upon him or herself to engender a critical consciousness in others. Rather, someone who recognises that development cannot be forced but only nurtured. The art of the development practitioner involves the facilitation of the emergent consciousness of others. Essentially, the development practitioner becomes an organisation development consultant, but to a select grouping of organisations – people's organisations, social movements, community-based organisations, non-governmental development organisations. He or she assists in the development of a healthy civil society which can serve to maintain a nation's consciousness, and, hopefully, hinders it from falling into the abuses of dogma, the unconsciousness of a status quo. Development work in this sense is the building of that civil society through the development of organisational capacity leading to the proliferation of organisation as such.

The discipline of organisation development is the building of organisational capacity in a very special sense. Interventions include training, skills transfer, evaluation, appropriate organisational design, and much more. But organisation development implies that interventions are brought to bear developmentally. That is, that organisations become more capable of maintaining and increasing their own capacity through their own self-reflective faculties. Learning organisations, organisations which through their own efforts remain at the cutting-edge of social transformation, are capable of self-analysis and self-reflection; this is the essence of self-regulation. Learning organisations are conscious organisations.

The development practitioner, then, becomes a facilitator of organisational consciousness. He or she needs to understand organisations and be able to bring experience to bear on issues. But, more particularly, he or she needs to understand the process of development in order to facilitate the 'stuck' organisation and organisational member into taking their next step, from whatever point they are at in the development process, through crisis and resistance to change, to a point of greater consciousness and awareness. And, as was indicated earlier, while the development practitioner needs expertise on organisation, a large part of the art of facilitation consists in the raising of questions. The art lies in finding the appropriate question which will serve to allow a group to confront their own unconscious assumptions and habits – and the implications of these – in order that the group can reflect, become conscious, and choose their next step in awareness and freedom. Awareness brings freedom, it brings control and real power; power not to coerce, but to act responsibly in the face of ambiguity and contradiction, to act out of oneself with initiative and creativity towards whatever is coming to one out of the future.

Summary

Our search for a new perspective on development does not imply a rejection of modernisation or political economy. The development of development theory is always 'as well as' rather than 'instead of'. The contradictions and dead-ends inherent in previous phases need to be incorporated, though transformed, in the subsequent phase.

The coercive notion of power in the independent phase of political economy requires transformation in the phase of interdependence. Thus power becomes the capacity to make decisions with maximum awareness. Development implies the ability to be objective and self-reflective; to transgress boundary lines between encampments; to raise questions about, rather than to enter into a new dependence on, new paradigms and ideologies; to move us to a new level of awakeness by breaking down newly formed boundaries and divisions in order that interdependence be recognised and struggled for.

For the individual, the phase of interdependence is equivalent to maturity. There is no greater learning ground for this than the contradictions and uncertainties inherent in organisational life. Thus interdependent consciousness is organisational consciousness. On the social level, the development of a strong civil society is the next phase in the development process – the step beyond independence to inter-dependence. The proliferation of competent people's organisations inherent in the notion of civil society thus contributes to the consciousness of individuals as well as to society as a whole, maintaining as it does the possibility of awakeness and fresh perspective in the face of the coercive dominance of state, capital and current paradigm. It is not a final answer; rather, it maintains and develops the ability to ask new questions.

As well, the crisis of meaning caused by progressive modernity and economic growth points to the proliferation of people's organisations as intermediate structures between the atomised individual and the order of the state (and capital) – civil society as the means for creating new meaning and reinstating non-economic value.

The development practitioner in this sense becomes the facilitator of the emergent consciousness of others, performed through developing the organisational capacity of civil society.

Interlude: Leadership

We sat on the hillside overlooking Wupperthal. Directly below us the river meandered lazily around the corner of the slope. From the river bank on the opposite side immaculate vegetable gardens spread themselves out until they reached the lines of white-washed cottages built precipitously on the far hill. The brownblack thatched roofs blended with the mountain; behind them, the rough stone walls of the animal pens were hardly to be distinguished from the natural rocky outcrops. Piet sat next to me in workers' overalls, his baseball cap worn, as always, the wrong way round on his head, the peak shading his back. It gave him an air of nonchalance, of irreverence, which contrasted with his position and the respect in which he was held. I loved him for it. He picked up another pebble and lobbed it casually out into space. We watched it curve away from us, saw its tumbling, turning fall and the small splash as it hit the water.

'The thing is this,' he said. 'Whatever decision I make, I'm the one who will be blamed. Because look, make no mistake, they may have given me the responsibility to make the decision, but everyone will resent me if I make it. Just because they ask me to do something which they can't do for themselves doesn't mean they'll accept my doing it.' He turned to me with a wry smile. 'You've been here long enough. You know what a strange people we are.'

'You're not,' I said. 'But that's beside the point anyway. Is there really no compromise which we could work out until the situation changes?'

Piet was the elected manager of the glove factory. This factory, which employed 70 villagers, had for years been run by the church's white contractor. All profits had accrued to him. Now the factory had been transformed into a workers' cooperative. While various worker committees controlled most of its affairs, Piet had been elected overall manager. He came from a small outstation situated some way from Wupperthal, through a gap in the hills. He had worked in the factory for years, had an acute intelligence and was well-liked. But leadership had not been his choice, and he was struggling to grow into the role. I had watched his natural humility grapple with his newfound stature, and knew that the challenge he faced now was a severe one.

'The thing is this,' he said. 'There is no compromise. The factory has faced this many times before. It's just that this is the first time we're faced with making the decision ourselves.'

66

The factory was dependent on two factors beyond its control. The first was supply. The leather used in the gloves was reject leather, and the tanneries supplied it only when available; they did not make it to order. The second was demand. These were industrial safety gloves, and the economic recession meant less demand and fewer sales. Already a mountain of gloves were lying unsold on the workshop floor. There was little leather with which to continue manufacturing, and little reason to do so anyway.

'I mean, we're not faced with the decision. I am.' The decision was not whether to close down or not. As Piet said, this had happened many times, and things always returned to normal, for a while at least. No, the problem was that for the foreseeable future the factory would only be able to justify three days' work per week. The decision which had to be made hinged around the fact that this was a cooperative in the service of the community. Should the factory reduce its workforce, lay off the younger members, and continue working a five-day week with a compliment of workers who had family responsibilities? Or should all members be retained, but on a three-day work schedule with proportionately less pay for everyone? The dilemma had split the entire community, for many families were dependent on factory wages. The debate had grown so hot, and so unresolved, that the cooperative had requested Piet to make the final decision on his own. He would not be financially affected either way as it was recognised that his job necessitated his working a five-day week in order to pull the factory back on track.

'Either way, some people in the community are going to lose. I live here, I have to live with that. I also have to think of what's best for the factory. The people no longer see that they all lose if the cooperative disintegrates. They only see their own need.' He took his cap off and ran a hand through his hair. He put his hand on my shoulder and looked at me resignedly. 'Leave me now, brother. You can't help me further with this one.'

I stood up, picked up his cap, put it back on his head the wrong way round, and picked my way down the slope to the plank bridge across the river.

5

A New Stance

Integration, Interdependence and Organisational Consciousness

When one has no character one has to apply a method.

Albert Camus, *The Fall*

If it is true that the development of people refers primarily to evolving consciousness, then any description of the development process necessarily entails a picture of emergent consciousness. Individually, organisationally and socially development implies the emergence of a new way of being in the world; a new thinking. The demands that this places on us and the possibilities it releases requires some elaboration. But consciousness does not lend itself easily to description. In its very nature as a state of supreme wakefulness, consciousness is mercurial, flexible, swift as a free-flowing river and as symbiotic as the play of sun and wind and cloud in the skies. It is almost impossible to capture. But it is necessary to form an image of what we are aiming towards.

We referred earlier to organisational consciousness. We talked of the phase of dependence as being characterised by a kind of unconsciousness, by uncritical acceptance, by a state of unity within a given status quo. We talked of the phase of independence as the beginning of the development process – a state of differentiation, division, separation and a defining of self as uniquely different from the other, the phase of critical consciousness. We moved on to talk of the phase of integration, of interdependence, of the simultaneous understanding of the reality of dependence with the necessity for independence: no longer unconsciousness or critical consciousness.

On one level 'organisational consciousness' is simply a term, a way of denoting a different form of consciousness. On another level, it forms a vital part of our understanding of this phase of development. One could as easily refer to it as interdependent consciousness, but I will talk of it as organisational consciousness for two reasons. Partly because it embodies the ability to maintain a wakeful state through holding the contradictions inherent in organisational life as a constant source of creativity through tension, in other words, not falling asleep into one or other extreme. And partly because the ability to function with consciousness within organisational reality demands the development of this new form of consciousness, this new stance.

To recap briefly: critical consciousness is a vital phase of the development process. But in itself it does not go far enough, not least because we tend to fall asleep in a new paradigm which is in opposition to others. Differentiation and division implies that where there was once unity there is now a conflict of opposites, and we risk falling asleep in one of the polarities. The challenge, though, is to stay awake. The development process is geared towards keeping us alive, supple, creative, and able to respond to the challenges of the future with new insights and activities, rather than with mindsets generated by, and appropriate to, the past or present.

The inevitable implication seems to be, then, that the integration phase is the reconciliation of opposites and the ability to compromise when faced with polarities. (Maturity is often – sometimes despairingly – regarded as the tendency to compromise on previously passionately held beliefs.) But to assume that the reconciliation of opposites in a spirit of compromise were the answer to the problems raised by the phase of independence would not do development justice. It is not reconciliation or compromise which is the essential note of organisational consciousness. Rather, it is the holding of the conflict between opposites *as conflict*. The ability to hold opposites as opposites, *in conflict*. Not to reconcile or compromise, but to see both as true at the same time, or at least to see both as embodying aspects of the truth.

Put slightly differently, we attempt to find harmony not through eradicating conflict but through dancing with conflict. We do not look for resolution of the conflict, but rather recognise the creativity which the conflict brings. We seek not compromise, but a living, continuously shifting balance by holding both polarities at once.

Some years ago I was asked whether I would consider consulting to a large non-governmental organisation. The organisation had not yet made up its mind whether or not I was the right consultant for them and I was called in for an initial interview with the group which was attempting to steer the development process of the organisation. The group consisted of about eight people, and tension was running through the room like open currents of electricity as I entered. I realised after a while that I was dealing here with two opposing factions, representative of what was going on in the organisation. Each faction had its own stories about what they had heard concerning my work as a consultant, and wanted confirmation or denial of these stories in order to be able to put their trust in me. One group clearly felt that their organisation was too 'democratic' for its own good, too informal and ad hoc. It was felt there were two few structures, too few formal decision-making procedures, too few accountability mechanisms and disciplining procedures. The leadership of the organisation was not strong enough, nor did they have enough hierarchically designated power. In the absence of all this, people were doing their own thing and the organisation was not producing. This group had heard that I pushed for more democratic functioning when I worked with organisations, that I promoted informality and had helped organisations to destructure themselves; that I was more concerned that leadership was accountable to staff than that staff were held accountable by leadership. Was this true, they asked?

The other group believed that the organisation was undemocratic, that it was led almost dictatorially from the top down, and that there was a highly structured hierarchy which maintained the status quo. Staff lacked the freedom to be creative and work developmentally; accountability mechanisms were bureaucratic, stifling and petty. Decision-making processes were not transparent; there were cliques who held power over other groupings. Staff felt oppressed and their grievances were ignored. This group had heard that in most of my work I helped organisations to structure themselves more tightly, formally, and specifically hierarchically. That I assisted organisations to formalise their accountability mechanisms. That generally I appeared to be in favour of organisations which tended towards bureaucracy, towards tight, formal structuring and strong leadership, towards curtailing staff freedom and creativity in favour of organisational regulations. Again, was this true, they asked?

All this emerged slowly. But where had all these impressions come from? Was my work really so opaque and so confusing? Eventually silence settled over the two groups and they waited expectantly for my response. I waited too, interested to see what it would be.

Then it came to me: all these stories were true. This was precisely the point. And so I gave them my answer. I told them that there were times when I appeared to help organisations in particular directions, and other times when it appeared that I was helping organisations in different directions. It all depended where the organisation was at the moment of intervention, and what was necessary at that point. They had been asking me what my 'hidden agenda' was when I intervened in organisational processes, whether I was promoting democracy, or structure, or hierarchy, or informality. I replied that I only had one agenda, and that was to help an organisation come to consciousness. I helped organisations reflect on themselves; I helped them to see how they were functioning, and to see this as objectively as possible. I tried to help organisations to draw out the contradictions in their behaviour; I tried to get them to look at the implications of their actions and the real consequences of their decisions. And when they were able to do this they came to their own conclusions about the way forward. Depending on where the organisation was at a particular time, solutions would differ, and different organisations would move in different directions. The results of my work then must indeed appear confusing, because the issue was not the particular choice that an organisation made but that the organisation made the correct choice in terms of, and for, itself; and that it made this choice in full awareness, in consciousness.

And the real task, I said, the real test and challenge was to help an organisation develop to the point where it had ways of maintaining this consciousness so that it did not fall asleep into the new solution, into a routine application of whatever decision had been made – for or against tighter structuring, or formalised hierarchy, or whatever. Arguing for either one of countless organisational polarities was to become trapped in the 'rigged debate', to circle round and round and miss the real issue. Which was that all these organisational polarities were both right and wrong. One had to balance them, not deny any of them even while making a choice for more of one or the other at a particular juncture. If I could help the organisation at all, I told them, it would be to bring them to a place where they could consciously and objectively choose the right path for themselves at that particular time, and then build ways of maintaining that consciousness so that they need not again fall asleep into a particular way of doing things, and particularly not fall asleep into the divisive and intensely polarised madness into which I had entered when the meeting had started earlier in the morning.

There are so many similar examples which can be drawn. The art of leadership, for instance. A major leadership skill consists in the ability to confront, to challenge, to discipline those whom it is one's responsibility to lead. Yet a completely contrasting skill is that of being able to support these same people, to nurture and develop them to their full potential. The ability to confront and the ability to support are opposing functions. The answer is not to compromise, but to be able to do both at the same time. To hold the tension between them, rather than to do less of each in order to find a middle way.

The development practitioner working with a community-based organisation is faced with a similar paradox. Expected to bring expertise and experience to bear on a particular problem, yet valued equally for the opposite ability to withhold this expertise while facilitating the organisation through its own process of developing its own ability to solve its own problems. Colleagues of mine worked with a community-based organisation which had received the advice of many fieldworkers from various non-governmental organisations during the preceding years, and which was struggling with various issues at the time. At the end of the organisational intervention the group thanked them by remarking on the difference they had experienced between the way my colleagues had worked and other fieldwork approaches which they had been exposed to. For the first time, they said, people had not come to them with advice, with their solutions and opinions. Rather my colleagues seemed to come with nothing except questions. They listened to the group, and through this and their questioning the group was able for the first time to really listen to itself.

Yet my colleagues remarked to me that it was not quite so simple; that they had in fact made suggestions and proffered tentative explanations which had helped to move the situation forwards. However, they had done it sensitively, and in such a way that the group's own insights about its situation were enhanced rather than eclipsed. And as with every such intervention, my colleagues were now exhausted and wanted to rest. The tension between facilitation and advice-giving is an intense one, and one which is not resolved through compromise; one needs to play with, rather than eradicate the conflict between, these two opposing modes of behaviour.

This is particularly applicable to development organisations which are constantly faced with potentially debilitating contradictions. For example, the contradiction between donor constraint and client needs. The contradiction between professionalism – with its hints of elitism, objectivity and formality – and the maintenance of informality with respect to grassroots relationships and linkages; the struggle for integrity between principle and strategy; the vexed question of the development organisation's relationship with the state; the contradiction between accountability for delivery, for product, and the fact that successful development work is entirely dependent upon the client's increasing ability to act; the need to plan and the need to remain open to community developments; the fact that successful development efforts generate new circumstances which often render the successful strategy no longer appropriate; the contradiction between service provision and development, between advice and facilitation. Within the realm of social process, every situation we face incorporates contradiction.

Heraclitus, a pre-Aristotelian Greek philosopher, maintained that conflict rather than peace is the cosmic principle of life; that all things come to pass through conflict. Creativity and life are the result of tension between opposites. He provides us with the example of the lyre, on which music is produced as a function of the tension in which the strings are held. Creativity and beauty through tension rather than relaxation, through conflict rather than through reconciliation. Harmony is attained not through resolution but through an attunement of opposite tensions – and the maintenance of that tension – like that in a bow. We must picture a bow ready strung but not in use. As it leans against the wall one sees no movement and thinks of it as a static object completely at rest. But in fact a continuous tug-of-war is going on within it, as will become evident if the string perishes. The bow will immediately take advantage, snap the string and leap to stretch itself. The source of the bow's power to shoot the arrow lies in the state of tension between opposites.

This tension is the source of life itself. Without the tension between opposites we could not be conscious. Slipping into one or other of two polarities renders us unconscious; it is the source of stagnation rather than creativity, of death rather than life. It heralds the supreme danger of fundamentalism, in which only one side of any polarity is recognised as having validity. Slipping into compromise does not bring resolution; the creative balance between black and white is not grey but rather the rainbow, the creative possibilities encompassed by holding both black and white as equally valid and by playing with the balancing of the tension between them.

I am calling this organisational consciousness because it is necessary for adequate organisational functioning, and because one of the most opportune places to learn it is through functioning healthily in organisations. As with the bow, it is a state of constant readiness to face and respond to the future. This is not easy to achieve or to maintain. A wakeful state requires constant vigilance and superlative effort in maintaining a perspective which is free enough to encompass both sides of an opposition; a perspective which is rooted in the recognition of paradox as reality. The phase of interdependence embodies the holding of a creative tension and balance between all opposites. It is the attempt to achieve unity through diversity.

This is the only state of being that is adequate for mastery over the two most basic challenges of development which face us as a society: the resolution of the conflict of opposites between freedom and responsibility, and between individuality and collectivism. With regard to the first, we need to achieve a balance between freedom from constraint on the one hand and the constraints upon action necessitated through recognising our responsibility for others (the consequences of our actions upon others). In other words, freedom to act without impinging upon others' freedom to act.

With regard to the second, we cannot allow the social nature of our humanity to be swamped by a rampant individualism. But neither can we allow the demands of collectivism to dictate to, or to thwart, individual creativity and initiative. We must find a creative balance between this tension of opposites. And it demands as well a balance between two further opposites: principle and expedient.

Anyone who has worked in organisations or in communities and who reflects honestly on their experience will recognise the necessity for balance between all extremes. They will recognise the unhealthy consequences of an ideological or practical bias towards either polarity, and will understand that there are no rules which serve to regulate the balance – which is not compromise but which is a living, subtle, adaptive blend of extremes in response to particular moments.

How do we begin to develop the capacity for this kind of flexible consciousness? One which is principled and which operates from the centre of one's being, but one which is also free to move and not trapped within its own blind spots.

People find this consciousness from many places. The ageing process itself often leads to maturity (although not if rigidity and opinionated prejudice entrench themselves). Organisational life is another training ground. Having someone external facilitate one through processes – which could be organisational, personal, or relational – is another way. And there are many others. I would like here, though, to use what we have already discovered about the development process to penetrate an aspect of this conscious suppleness and flexibility. I believe there are elements in the development process which are both instructional and central.

We observed that the development process is discontinuous, that it moves 'stepwise' rather than in a continuous upward curve, and that the move between steps is often precipitated – or perhaps one should say mediated – by crisis. When we characterise the different phases of development we risk missing the most important aspect of the process: the place in between the different stages, the process of transition itself. The place where one has let go of the old in order to embrace the new. That place of bewilderment, casting about in the dark, nothing known to lean on, no familiar footsteps in which to put one's feet. That place of chaos, the liminal space in between worlds.

How many times I have worked with organisations which were afraid to let go of the old, but which eventually did so, not because a new dispensation had been worked out but in order to be free to work one out. Each time resistances arose because people wanted answers before they would be prepared to change, and were not able to accept that the answers would continue to elude them until they let go and threw themselves into the chaos of transition, with no guarantee – apart from faith in themselves and in those helping them – that the answers would come. And in that transition process, which for some organisations can last months, nothing is certain: authority, structure, procedure, strategy, or individual future. I have the utmost awe, respect and admiration for those organisations prepared to go through the eye of the needle. It is the only developmental option we have, but this does not make it any easier. I regard with wonder too the many individuals who successfully negotiate this dark and bewildering process of transformation, and am privileged to be part of an entire nation which has proved big enough to let go of the old and enter a process of transition with no guarantee of security on the other side.

There are many capacities which individuals and organisations require to be considered capable. Organisations, for example, need a coherent and sensible vision, effective strategies and strategic planning systems, appropriate structures and procedures, good leadership, expertise as well as human resource development processes. But I am more and more convinced that what differentiates the really capable organisation or individual from others is one primary capacity: the ability to move. This is the key, and the distinguishing feature of the conscious organisation and individual. The ability to move between polarities and not to get fixated and stuck. To have the courage and the strength to walk these ambiguous and uncertain canyons in vulnerability and openness.

We are hindered by cultures which celebrate the light and the certainty of the sun. By cultures which do not respect vulnerability, but which reward people for the speed and certainty of their answers rather than for their questions and doubts. To shoot first and ask questions later is an independent stance; interdependence demands more humility, but is little understood. Many dark nights spent lying in the mountains looking at the stars have not lessened my sense of wonder at the fact that these same stars are there all the time, but during the day the vision of this mysterious and gently studded universe is obliterated by the confident power of a dominant sun. Until we can wander in the dark, embrace the chaotic uncertainty of the spaces of transition which lie between the worlds of certainty and action, until then we will not be able to embrace the freedom of movement necessary to a state of interdependent or organisational consciousness.

Yet there is a rich thread of tradition which does acknowledge the centrality of chaos and uncertainty. The Old Testament story of the Ten Commandments provides one illustration. When Moses first brought the commandments down from the mountain he beheld the people of Israel praying to a golden calf, and in his despair he shattered the tablets. In the midst of this despair he was commanded to return to the summit and continue his work, not knowing any more whether there was any point. The people of Israel accepted the commandments on his second descent, and an ark was built to house the tablets. What is most illustrative for us in this story is the fact that this ark was built big enough to house not only the tablets containing the commandments but the original broken tablets as well. These fragments of the shattered tablets were thus honoured and carried into the future, as both a reminder and a symbol of the value of process, the value of the dark and broken times of the human spirit.[1]

Robert Johnson draws on the mythology of the Innuit people to illuminate a similar point. He writes the following:

> An Eskimo shaman's tale gives a clue: The good spirits needed a new shaman in an Eskimo community to replace the old shaman who had died. They chose an adolescent boy to be trained for this role. They took him into the underworld and cut him up into pieces so that no two bones touched each other. Then the evil spirits came and gnawed all the flesh from the exposed bones. When the future shaman was completely gnawed bare and not one bone touched another, the good spirits returned, put all the bones back together again ... put new flesh on his reconstructed bones, and welcomed him into the tribe as the new shaman. A record was kept of all the evil demons who had gnawed on his bones, since the new shaman had the power to cure any illness caused by such demons. He was unable to cure any illness caused by an evil demon that was not present at his dismemberment.
>
> This ... is the preparation for consciousness [our modern word for shaman power] and the suffering is the training for the future healer or genius.[2]

Robert Bly asserts that it is through the wounds which one has sustained, through the hurt that one has suffered, that people reach maturity, strength and consciousness. 'Some old traditions say that no man is adult until he has become opened to the soul and spirit world, and they say that such an opening is done by a wound in the right place...'[3] Lievegoed notes that consciousness is found on the boundaries of the shattered soul.[4]

All this may seem slightly esoteric, but it nevertheless attests to the same wisdom: that organisational consciousness and interdependence – as a holding and living with the creative tension between opposites, as the maintenance of a wakeful state by not falling asleep into one or other polarity – demands mobility, suppleness and flexibility. The ability to negotiate these strange and sometimes terrifying spaces which we would all rather do without is the key to consciousness. The development process is not simply the various phases through which we pass, but the act of transformation contained in the journey through that place of transition between the phases. Development is an adventure in search of consciousness, and no adventure is true without its share of pain, despair and uncertainty.

As a global community we appear to have reached the stage of independence, and are only now, in facing the crises precipitated by the excesses of this stage, struggling to move beyond. We are searching for a new stance, a new way of thinking. The dependence stage is characterised by a relatively unconscious harmony and sense of unity; a sense of belonging within a framework which is given and which is full of meaning and interconnectedness: we are an indivisible part of a whole. Indigenous peoples reveal to us the extent of our loss in this regard (and while development entails loss, it also entails the transformation of this lost element in later phases).

The phase of independence, as applied to the faculty of thought, marks the advent of logic and of dualistic thinking. Logic involves the paradigm of cause and effect, of division and separation. The basis of logic is categorisation: if something belongs in one category, it cannot at the same time belong in its opposite category. Concepts are mutually exclusive. Logic cannot deal with the resolution of opposites. It is the ideal tool for the phase of independence; it tolerates no ambiguity.

Logic is a vital and important phase in the development of thought. It forms the basis of science, and without it we would not be able to live as we do today; without it the industrial revolution and subsequent material advances would not have been possible. Logical thinking has proved to be highly seductive primarily because it works; it has given us control of our world and hence independence. Yet increasingly it is recognised, within the realm of science, that while logic works admirably in many areas, it does not work on the micro-level (the level of quantum physics), nor on the macro-level (the level of astronomy). In both these areas, uncertainty, unpredictability and the identity of opposites are having to be taken into account.

We are increasingly seeing that logic also does not work in the social realm, in the realm of organisations and communities. Here too, uncertainty, unpredictability and the identity of opposites are having to be recognised. The social problem of alienation too, of lack of meaning, cannot be resolved through logic. Logic, indeed, renders meaning unnecessary and, in fact, meaningless. We need to recreate the sense of meaning which was such an integral, if unconscious, part of life in a transformed and conscious manner.

The key to consciousness is a new way of thinking. Dualistic thinking will no longer suffice, and we need to cultivate three-fold thinking – the unity of opposites in a greater whole. This is not a state which can be maintained indefinitely in all areas of our lives as development is a cyclical process and we continually slip back into routine reliance on a given paradigm.

Langer, in a wonderful exposition on what she calls 'mindfulness', indicates how we continually slip back into mindlessness, and notes that the three key qualities to a mindful state of being are the creation of new categories, the openness to new information, and the ability to be aware of more than one perspective.[5] Lievegoed talks of the fact that, while we used to search for the truth, our search is now for the 'good', a recognition of the fact that the 'good' is not ultimate truth but is conditional upon circumstance; what is good in certain circumstances is not necessarily so in others.[6] What is demanded, then, is wakefulness; awareness of consequences and implication of actions; the ability to forge new meaning in the absence of rules and given norms; and thus the capacity for self-reflection. Finally, under these conditions, there can be no substitute for personal integrity and respect for others – without these, the advent of three-fold thinking heralds a bleak future indeed.

For the masses of ordinary people unexposed to the privileged realms of esoteric science, the development process will take place within the realm of organisation, the most engaging form of social reality. Organisation challenges and involves the whole person. Not simply the realm of thought, but the realms of feeling and action as well. In order to function adequately within an organisational context, the individual must develop a sense of interdependence, maturity and flexibility.

The development process is a progressive – but discontinuous – advance to greater consciousness. The ability to be awake and aware. There is no other solution available to us. Consciousness is not a reconciliation or a compromise of opposites; it is the ability to work with opposites constructively and draw creativity from tension and conflict; it is consciously balanced action. It is a supreme challenge which we will only achieve intermittently. But each intermittent achievement will make subsequent ones easier. As Fry so eloquently noted, 'It takes so many thousand years to wake; but will you wake, for pity's sake.'[7]

Summary

Interdependence heralds a form of three-fold thinking which embodies a new stance towards the world. While dependence is characterised by a relatively unconscious and uncritical acceptance of a particular status quo as given, and independence by critique, differentiation and a defining of self as uniquely different from other, interdependence necessitates the simultaneous holding of the reality of dependence with the necessity for independence. Interdependent, or organisational, consciousness is the ability to stay awake, alive, supple and creative; the ability to respond to the challenges of the future with new insights and activities rather than with mindsets generated by, and appropriate to, the past or present.

Consciousness in this sense is a new way of thinking. It is not reconciliation or compromise, it is the holding of the conflict, the tension, between opposites as conflict and tension. We seek not compromise but a living balance by holding both polarities at once. Harmony and creativity are attained not through resolution but through an attunement of opposite tensions – and the maintenance of that tension – like that in a strung bow. The source of the bow's power to shoot the arrow lies in the state of tension between opposites, between the tautly pulled string and the tensely bent wood. This tension is the source of life itself. It is consciousness. It is a state of constant readiness to face, and respond to, the future.

This is the only stance which is adequate to achieving mastery over the two fundamental challenges of development: the contradictions between freedom and responsibility, and between individuality and collectivism. It is a stance which demands integrity because it requires a balance between two further opposites: principle and expedient. It is a new way of thinking: three-fold as opposed to dualistic thinking.

Organisational consciousness can be learned through achieving competency in organisational life. The level of organisational consciousness prevalent in a particular society will be a reflection of the strength and extent of civil society.

Interlude: Organisation

It had been quite some journey getting here through the wild winter storm, for the roads which clung precariously to the mountain sides were a muddy slush, and my arms ached from continuous wrenching of the steering wheel as tyres slithered dangerously close to the abyss. The rivers were in flood, and on leaving Wupperthal the lights of the van had twice dipped below the water level as I fought the vehicle against the raging current and the loose stony river bottom, leaving me for moments in utter panic at the pitch black night. Yet I had made it through the storming blackness, and miraculously all the others had made it too. We were 20 men sitting shoulder to shoulder in a tiny room in a tiny outlying village, two candles flickering on a wooden table and a paraffin lamp hanging from a nail in the wall. Outside the rain drummed against the window panes and the wind howled between the mountain peaks. The powerful, squat old man spoke again, more emphatically this time, the grey stubble on his chin lit by candle light.

'Mr Kaplan here keeps telling us about the advantages of working together. Yet he is not a rooibos farmer; he has never farmed in his life. And the one thing we need, the use of the processing barn in Wupperthal, he cannot get for us. I say we continue working with our own families. I have never been beholden to anyone, and I'm not about to throw in my lot with some of you.'

There were some murmurs of assent, but most of the men kept silent. Slowly a long beanpole of a man disentangled himself from the shadows, stepped across the bodies and approached the table in the centre. His clothes hung on him as from a hanger and his face, lit by the candle from beneath, was a hawk-like etching of light and shadow. He spoke slowly, looking around him at each upturned face with an air of quiet purpose.

'Everything that brother Bokkie says is true. Yet it is a truth which keeps us in bondage and does not allow us the privilege of risk. For Bokkie, nothing should change. Yet we are stuck, and we know we are, otherwise we would not be here tonight.' He coughed into his hand, a dry, hacking cough, before continuing: 'Look. Look at us. Each of us in our villages, we farm on our own, transport on our own, struggle with the Rooibos Control Board on our own, yet day by day we get poorer together. We cannot challenge the white farmers for a decent share of the market because each of us on our own has nothing. If we organised together, if we overcame the barriers that separated us, we could pool resources, gain power, challenge the discrimination practised against us by the Control Board because we are coloured and because we are poor.'

The grizzled old man called Bokkie made as if to speak again, but the speaker raised his hand and quieted him. 'Wait. I have not finished. I am not used to speaking. Have the decency to hear me out.' Again came the dry, hacking cough. 'The key to our organising is the use of the processing barn. The church, without giving reasons, denies us permission to use it. Yet it would change everything for us. Brother Bokkie is right when he says that Mr Kaplan has not been able to persuade the church. But he misunderstands the point of Mr Kaplan's being here among us, of all the long conversations we have had with him, the questions which he has forced upon us.' A smile flickered across his face for a moment and then disappeared, like a trick of the candle light. 'If we form an association of rooibos farmers, the association will be able to put more pressure on the church than any one of us alone. Together, we can simply occupy the barn if need be, which we could not do alone. And with the barn in our possession we would be in a position to start to make something of our farming.'

He stood still for some moments, looked around him slowly, then retreated back to the shadows. A hand rose, and a young, open-eyed man spoke.

'I don't understand. How would we share profits and losses? How could I be sure that others are working as hard as I am? If we bought a tractor, who would get the use of it?'

I got to my feet tentatively. 'May I speak?' A number of heads nodded. 'There are many questions which we do not have the answers to now. There are various different routes available, and different choices which could be made. We would have to put our heads together and work these things through. But we cannot do this unless we can decide in principle whether it makes sense to organise together or not. Are we willing to try it, or would we rather continue on our own?'

A hum of voices broke out, temporarily silencing the pervasive drumming of the rain. I felt the one called Bokkie staring hard at me across the room. When eventually he rose and stilled the room as he began to speak, I was struck, as always before, by the raw strength of the man.

'Let's do it,' he said. 'Long Jan is right. Mr Kaplan is not a farmer, but we know little about organising. I'm prepared to see what will happen if we put the two together. But', he added, glaring around the room, 'we will need to work this thing out in very fine detail before I join hands with anyone.'

Many hours later, when eventually we filed out of that smoke-filled room, the ice-cold night air hit us like an express train, knocking the breath out of us. The rain had ceased, the wind sunk to little more than a whisper, and we stood around talking quietly, breathing deeply of that brilliant black night in the mountains.

6

The Practice of the Development Practitioner

A great mutual embrace is always happening
between the eternal and what dies,
between essence and accident.

Rumi, *Breadmaking*

As their essential task, development practitioners assist in bringing individuals, organisations and societies to power. They intervene in people's processes such that they are able to realise their power, and, ultimately, enable people to act out of a centre of awareness and objectivity. Development practitioners collaborate with people in the claiming of their rights, and facilitate their recognition of responsibilities. They facilitate their development towards a more human, purposeful and conscious future, and work through organisations and communities towards the actualisation of a conscious society.

A high task indeed, and one which has not been accorded its due recognition. Partly, I suspect, because the task of the development practitioner has not been adequately understood. More importantly, however, because agreeing about the task raises major questions about practice.

There are many different kinds of development practitioner operating out of, and on, vastly different situations. The variety of practices is so broad, and so eclectic, that it is small wonder that there is little coherent picture of the practice available. There has been little to guide either the practitioner or the development organisation out of which the practitioner operates. I would contend, though, that this does not have to be the case, and that we have paid the discipline too little respect in our failure to adequately think things through. In particular, we have underconceptualised development itself, and thus underconceptualised the practice of the development practitioner.

I do not intend to get involved here in a discussion about the various methodologies and techniques which are available to the practitioner. They are many – rapid rural appraisal, participatory rural appraisal, participatory research, community mapping, strategic planning, vision building, cooperative development, various forms of problem identification and analysis, project planning and implementation, project monitoring and evaluation, to name but a few. These, relevant and useful though they may be, are not what concern us here. I mean something different by 'the practice of the development practitioner'. How do we describe this work? Whatever techniques or methodologies the practitioner uses, what is it that he or she is actually doing? What is the practitioner's approach?

Our starting point lies in understanding the process of development itself. It is against the background of all that we have observed concerning the development process that I would like to characterise the practice of the development practitioner. That this practice consists of many seemingly contradictory, and certainly diverse, strategies and activities does not imply that 'anything goes'. On the contrary, an appreciation of development imposes an intelligent and intelligible framework on the variations of practice.

We referred earlier to the development practitioner as alternatively apolitical welfare worker, activist, fieldworker assisting communities towards self-reliance, and organisation development consultant (to the 'organs' of civil society). All of these approaches call for different strategies and activities, and they often consist of contradictory approaches. Yet the practitioner engages in most of them to some degree; it all depends on the demands of the situation. More particularly, it depends on the practitioner's reading of the developmental phase which is being addressed. However, this reading seldom takes place; moreover the practitioner – and development organisation – often fails to differentiate between different approaches. The result is gross confusion and real contradiction rather than fine discrimination.

The development practitioner as welfare worker seems a misnomer, and indeed runs the risk of increasing, rather than decreasing, dependence. Thus the welfare worker is the least sensible use of the term development practitioner. Yet there can be no doubt that the practitioner brings resources to the client community which this community might lack in and of itself, even if only with respect to previous experience and an outsider's perspective. Something is brought, something given to the situation, and there are times when resources – perhaps financial or material – can assist, rather than detract from, the shift from dependence to independence. Generally this is a dangerous intervention, if we consider development the task at hand, because it can lead to increased dependence. But I have seen situations where, for example, community organisations genuinely required office space and equipment for their further development towards independence. The development practitioner or funder who scorns the welfare approach regards this kind of request as irrelevant, if not ignoble and potentially detrimental. And perhaps it is. Yet the developing organisation requires resources, and at times can develop beyond this need through having them provided rather than withheld on the grounds that such a response is non-developmental. It all depends on a fine reading of the situation at hand.

There are times too when the development practitioner must function as activist. We have already seen that development implies radical structural transformation of an existing system. Certainly this is true of the shift from dependence to independence. Empowerment and consciousness are all very well but there are times when economic, political and social structures – the prevailing status quo – so militate against independence that changes to these structures on the macro level become a necessary precondition for emancipation and independence. Put another way, development is constrained when the context within which it is being pursued is severely disabling.

The development practitioner as activist on behalf of others runs the same risk as the welfare worker: that of increasing dependence on the practitioner. Certainly the ideal way is to enable the community, society or client grouping to find their own power through encouraging and facilitating their own activism. This should be the way of the development practitioner if all that we have observed about the development process is true. But there are instances when the practitioner can intervene helpfully in order to free a situation sufficiently for the next advance towards power to be made. Once again it depends on a fine reading of the development trajectory of the client grouping for the relevant intervention to be made at the appropriate time.

Ultimately the task is to facilitate an increase in the power and consciousness of social groupings. To leave them in a better condition than they were in before, with more capacity to control their world, their context and themselves. But particularly to maintain a condition of awareness and to be able to respond creatively and responsibly to approaching challenges. We arrive then at a picture of the practice of the development practitioner as being the facilitation of the development of people's organisations; the facilitation of the institutional capacity of those institutions forming the building blocks of civil society. Whether we talk of rural or urban development, community development or the development of specific sectors such as health, agriculture or human rights, the development of a society might be measured through the competence and extent of its organisational capacity. It is organisation which mediates between 'macro' and 'micro' elements of society; and it is through organisation that the individual comes to grips with the structural and policy levels of societal functioning. The measure of the consciousness of a society will be the level of civil organisation which it is able to achieve. Sheldon Annis, tabulating some successes of development in Latin America, says, 'If anything is certain about the nature of "grassroots organisations", it is that ... they are *not* homogenous units ... Yet, setting aside ... [their differences] ... the important point is this: even though organisations appear and disappear with sometimes astonishing rapidity, organisation has become relatively constant in Latin America over the past twenty or so years.'[1]

Piers Campbell, in discussing the concept of institutional development as the most important focus of development work, puts this argument very succinctly:

'Institutional development is both a development strategy and an organisational development intervention. As a development strategy, institutional development aims to promote and facilitate the establishment of a thriving community of local development institutions. As an organisational development intervention, institutional development assists local institutions to become more effective, viable, autonomous and legitimate.'[2]

In other words, the development practitioner is to facilitate the development of community-based organisation. If we take the discipline of organisation development as the facilitation of an organisation's capacity to self-reflect, self-regulate, and take control of its own processes of improvement and learning, then we can also affirm that the essential work of the development practitioner is to facilitate the consciousness of individuals, communities and nations through the medium of people's organisations.

Thus we have the concept of the development fieldworker, whose task is to facilitate the growing capacity of the organisations which constitute civil society. Particularly community-based membership organisations and non-profit, non-governmental organisations concerned with social transformation, resource allocation, development and access to power (in other words, what are sometimes called 'value-based organisations'). The actual practice of such fieldworkers should depend on the development situation which they are responding to. There are thus various forms of fieldwork, from unstructured and informal 'community development' work through to highly structured and contained consultancy processes with formal contracts. Development organisations and practitioners often do not distinguish between different fieldwork practices and interventions because they lack the conceptual framework within which to understand the development processes to which they are responding.

For example, the community in which no organisation or in which only quasi-organisation exists, or the community which is acquiescent and dependent, requires leadership and motivation, a galvanising activity. Pure facilitative fieldwork may not be appropriate where there is no groundswell of activity to facilitate. Here the practitioner needs to work more as animator, as activist, in order to provide the leadership which is lacking, to provide 'voice' in the midst of what has come to be regarded – following Freire – as the oppressed's 'culture of silence'. Yet later, when organisation has been established and has attained a certain degree of capacity, when the community or social grouping has moved from the phase of dependence into a more independent state, this same attitude will come across as paternalistic and patronising, and will in fact often hold the group back from further development. The very attitude and practice which helped facilitate development at one stage becomes detrimental at another.

Even later, when a community is more 'sophisticated' and has attained a larger degree of organisation, and when discrete organisations are functioning as expressions of the group's independence and capacity, the unstructured and informal nature of community development fieldwork which works so well during the organisation building phase may become detrimental, when it no longer accords with the growing formality and differentiation – independence – of the community or organisation with which it is working, it once again finds itself out of step with real needs. Community development fieldworkers tend to value informality while organisational consultants prefer to work within the framework of formal contracts. While informality facilitates interaction with less 'developed' organisations and communities, it often keeps control of the process in the hands of the fieldworker. Part of the organisation's or social grouping's process of development lies in its ability to take control of the interventions which it requests; setting the terms of reference and defining the framework. This is the domain of the development practitioner as 'consultancy fieldworker' rather than 'community development fieldworker'.

During the phase of dependence, then, fieldwork will consist in part of resource provision and activism. As independence is attained these components should diminish, and their place be taken by the provision of training, the facilitation of the clients' coming into their own power, and the building of organisational capacity. The move to interdependence implies that many of these things have already been attained, and the practitioner will function more as a contracted organisation development consultant, facilitating the ability of organisations to self-reflect, self-regulate, and take control of their own processes of improvement and learning. Throughout, the emphasis is on facilitating the development of consciousness, and this will take different forms of practice depending on the stage which the client has reached during its own process of development.

It should be clear then that there is no single way to practice development; that development takes time and energy; that there is no end to the development process; and that the relationship between practitioner and client is marked by shifts in attitudes and strategies. Once one begins to understand and appreciate the development process itself then it becomes possible to differentiate the various different forms of practice and the various different strategies which the practitioner must be capable of employing. Fine powers of observation and the ability to interpret what is seen are necessary to respond in a fashion appropriate to the development needs of a particular time and place. This is the case whether we are looking at the development of communities, social groupings, organisations or individuals. We will touch briefly on each of these in turn in order to illustrate and expand upon the points raised above.

Insofar as community work is concerned, there are times when the practitioner would do best to leave the situation alone completely. When a community is content with its lot, and where no questions are being asked or tensions expressed, it is perhaps better to leave the situation as it is found. Any intervention is an intrusion, especially as any developmental leap involves the pain of loss, the loss itself, and an increase in complexity and ambiguity. Can we presume, as practitioners, that in situations such as just described, where we may not have been asked in by the people concerned, our interventions and the people's development will be to their own advantage, even in the long-term? We need to tread carefully; these are people's lives that we are dealing with.

When the phase of independence is entered, there is another scenario that often manifests itself. I have regularly heard community development fieldworkers complain about the conflict that is rife in communties, and that seems to get worse, rather than easier, as the development 'project' progresses. They complain about selfishness, about people doing things for their own gain (even under the auspices of the development project), and about the formation of cliques and power groupings. They resent the fact that this is happening when they themselves are motivated to do the work they do for the 'social good', and for the sake of the community as a whole. On the other side many enterprising community members complain that the fieldworkers are only prepared to help cooperative groups and not individuals, that these groupings do not work, and that those who are motivated and enterprising – even if only for their own gain – should lead and reap the benefits of development.

Understanding the process of development should give us insight into these issues. The divisiveness and differentiation they express, the conflict and tension, the emphasis on the individual rather than on the collective (in the face of the fieldworker's desperate attempts to talk 'community') all point to the manifestation of the phase of independence. These things should be expected, rather than met with shock and horror by well-meaning practitioners. Development projects should take them into account and plan around them, rather than impose on them an outsider's rigid ideological grid and set of principles. We are dealing with process, with time, with resistances, with developmental sequences, and one of the greatest dangers in our work lies in dictating from the developmental point that *we* have reached rather than responding to a reading of the development process of our clients.

In another scenario, community-based organisations, as they develop through independence to the possibility of inter-dependence – with other organisations and communities – often tend to lose touch with their constituencies and with the membership base which they should be responding to. As the organisation becomes more sophisticated it becomes more complex, and demands expertise, speed of decision and flexibility. These requirements often distance it from the mass of members who used to play an integral role in its functioning. Once more, there is nothing to be alarmed at; this is all part of the development process. This is not to say that nothing need be done about the situation. On the contrary, this is what the development practitioner is there for. But the process cannot be fought. It must be worked through intelligently, and should be facilitated.

These abbreviated examples bring us to the realm of organisation. Here too the practitioner needs to be able to 'see' the development phase which is being struggled with if interventions are to be helpful. We saw earlier how organisations move through the phases of development on their path of becoming. I would like now to look at the same pattern from another perspective.

Experience in working with organisations reveals that there are certain requirements placed on the functioning of organisations which call themselves healthy or capacitated. First comes the development of a conceptual framework which reflects the organisation's understanding of the world. Organisations which do not have a competent working understanding of their world can be said to be incapacitated, regardless of how many other skills and competencies they may have. A second requirement concerns organisational attitude. An organisation needs to build its confidence to act in and on the world in a way in which it believes it can be effective and have an impact. Ultimately it also needs to accept responsibility for the social and physical conditions 'out there'. This implies a shift from the critical mode to a more interdependent frame. With clarity of understanding and a sense of confidence and responsibility comes the possibility of developing organisational vision and strategy.

Although these requirements are not gained entirely sequentially, we may say that once organisational aims and strategy are clear it becomes possible to structure the organisation in an appropriate fashion. Form follows function – if one tries to do this the other way around the organisation becomes incapacitated. The next step in the march towards organisational capacity is the growth and extension of individual skills, abilities and competencies; the traditional terrain of training courses. Once again, while these requirements overlap, there does appear to be a sequence. The organisation which does not know where it is going and why, which has a poorly developed sense of responsibility for itself, and which is inadequately structured, cannot make use of training courses and skills aquisition – they simply do not hold.

Finally, an organisation needs material resources. Without an appropriate level of these the organisation will always remain, in an important sense, incapacitated.

Clearly there are many differentiated strategies needed to respond to these requirements. It is interesting to note that, while the above may be an accurate description of the sequential requirements for organisational capacity, woe betide the development practitioner who follows such a prescriptive listing slavishly, using it as a lens through which to view organisational issues. As a diagnostic framework and a set of guidelines it may be useful, but the practitioner who does not read the organisation carefully in terms of its current developmental phase will do more harm than good.

Organisations repeat phases at different stages of their developmental process. Whether an organisation is young (in the pioneer phase), or reaching the point of differentiation which marks the phase of independence, or working out of a renewed sense of interdependence between the individual and the collective, will have profound implications for the way in which it struggles with the requirements for organisational functioning mentioned above. For example, while the new organisation will need clarity of vision, it may not yet have the problems which accompany vision-building activities within older organisations. The needs of different staff members in terms of skills aquisition will differ at different stages of the organisation's life, as will material resource constraints and needs. Similarly, with respect to structure, organisations will have different needs at different stages of their lives. At times an increasingly complex structure is called for; at other times 'destructuring' is required.

The needs of, and constraints on, different organisational 'attitudes' or 'cultures' will also vary according to where the organisation is with respect to its development process. To mention one example, there are times when a more action-oriented culture is necessary, while at other times this may be detrimental and a more reflective culture of monitoring and evaluation is appropriate. The issue is not to lay prescriptions down on organisations, but to understand where the organisation is and to help it through the transition to the next step which is appropriate for it. The task is always to facilitate greater consciousness on the part of the organisation so that it can find its own next step. Variations in practice should respond to this task.

Organisational needs will also differ in terms of the kind of organisation. There are vast differences in need between membership organisations with paid staff and membership organisations without; between small organisations and large organisations; between local organisations and national organisations with regional branches; between individual organisations and organisational associations or networks. The requirements tabled above for healthy organisations remain, but the way they are applied will differ. Good practice is the application of such guidelines with due respect to the organisation's ability to come to greater awareness of itself, greater consciousness and therefore greater control, creativity and responsibility. All this has major implications for development practice. I shall raise these instances of practice here.

A development organisation focusing on early childhood educare (ECE), in a developing country where the state makes no provision for such services, sets itself the task of facilitating the development of autonomous ECE centres in marginalised and disadvantaged communities – centres which will be owned and controlled by the community. At the same time it performs 'activist' work of lobbying for changes to national educational policy which will advantage the ECE sector. Recognising that the centres are severely incapacitated with respect to both organisational as well as educational competence, it works to remedy this situation. It believes that skills are lacking, and necessary. So it undertakes to provide appropriate training. Accordingly, it employs trainers to run training programmes in organisation, administration, finance, as well as in teaching methodology. The idea is to train teachers who will be employed by trained community committees.

Twelve years later the organisation can justifiably claim to be serving over 100 pre-school centres, some in relatively far-flung rural areas. Yet of all these centres, only a handful are autonomous or independent, and these are situated in middle-class areas. The rest are entirely dependent on the development organisation's provision, and are, in any event, unstable and largely organisationally incoherent. Committees are barely functioning and turnover of teachers is high; financial autonomy is a distant dream, not even entertained by many of the centres.

What has gone wrong? A crisis in the organisation leads to an analysis of the situation. It transpires that a number of the community workers have been signalling for some time that something is amiss: centres are not progressing towards autonomy; training does not seem to be working; fieldworkers themselves appear under, or inappropriately, skilled. Those at the organisational centre – the training coordinators, the specialist trainers, the lobbyists, the leaders – have refused to heed the lessons coming in from the field; refused to adapt their practice or critique their paradigm. Vested interests (apart from having fallen asleep into an unconscious reliance on a particular theory) make them resistant to change. Trainers' security is threatened; lobbyists have publicly put themselves on the line in propagation of a specific educational philosophy; leaders' reputations are at stake.

Confronting itself honestly at last, the organisation develops an understanding concerning the reasons for failure, which proves illuminating.

The centres are based in communities which are marginalised in many ways, lack of education and unemployment being not the least of these. The delivery of training packages, mostly performed on the development organisation's premises, is not working because there is not enough follow-up in the field and because skills are not the primary issue; they are necessary but not sufficient. The centres have far more debilitating issues to cope with which include the following: committee members seldom find the time to attend meetings and consequently there is no real 'pioneering leadership' for the new centres; formal relationships between the community, parents, the committees and the teachers (in all their combinations) are unclear and confused; committee members elected for a term of office come to the end of their term just as they are gaining competence; teachers are poorly paid and have to moonlight or leave to seek work elsewhere; the development organisation's training packages are inappropriate to local context or particular levels of education, and both teachers and committees are experiencing problems which can find no resolution through training; active members of the community are more concerned with their political struggle for rights than with running pre-schools; the centres lack a coherent sense of vision and strategy, and there is conflict around various alternative approaches; and finally organisational experience and discipline are lacking and centres are not able to self-reflect and self-regulate their practice.

It is then understood by the organisation that the provision of training has become an end in itself, and that the focus of practice is on the number of training courses run rather than on the emergence of genuinely autonomous pre-school centres. A new approach is clearly needed, and one which puts the emphasis on the centres; that is, development rather than a training approach is necessary. And development practitioners in the field, rather than trainers, are required to put it into effect. Such development practitioners should work intensively with specific centres, assisting them to reflect on their practice, to resolve interpersonal conflict, to renew their aims and objectives, to problem solve and come up with appropriate strategies for resolution of issues, to restructure themselves where necessary, to engage in planning processes and ongoing evaluation, monitoring and supervision. Only once this work has been done can specific training needs be ascertained and specific training packages utilised. Trainers should thus service, and work in support of, fieldworkers (whereas the dominant paradigm had always emphasised the opposite). Development practitioners would not be delivering products but would be facilitating organisation development processes aimed at strengthening the institutional capacity of these organs of civil society.

This example serves to illustrate the difference between a practice which emphasises the provision of a service based on assumptions around the service itself, and a far more developmental practice with differentiated strategies based on an objective and intelligent reading of the developmental trajectory and needs of the client. (Needless to say, these transformations in practice were accompanied by very painful development processes within the organisation itself, which had its effect on all of the various strategies, on structures and roles, on human resource development, and on personal futures.)

In another example and following the transition process in South Africa, a national education project with enormous financial resources decides it would like to assist in the upgrading of historically disadvantaged schools. Recognising that the problems faced by these schools are manifold, it adopts a sensibly holistic approach which it terms 'whole school development', and offers schools the finances they need to buy in the services of various educational development organisations which provide different methodologies for addressing the schools' needs.

The national project, however, has lost some perspective on the various elements needed to capacitate the schools. It stipulates that the money can only be accessed once effective community governance structures are in place (to ensure adequate and responsible leadership), and that the money can only be used for human resource development with respect to certain limited school subjects, as well as management training. The schools will not be able to use the money for anything other than this, and certainly not for material resources (which were recognised as being a need but not a priority for the development of organisational capacity).

The project's intention was honourable, but from a developmental point of view it was both overprescriptive and underconceptualised. Overprescriptive because assumptions were made about what individual schools needed and a sequence of provision was dictated without anyone ever having surveyed the actual schools in question. Underconceptualised because, while there was an attempt at a developmental response, the actual functioning of development processes was never thought through. Thus the various services offered were inappropriate to meeting the individual needs of the different schools at their different stages of development, and the schools felt that they had no say over the process of development prescribed for them, and were thus resentful and uncooperative. Because they had not been facilitated through a process of becoming conscious of their own contradictions and had not articulated for themselves the demands of their own development pathways, they could make no sense or effective use of community governance structures. Management training seemed irrelevant to them while they suffered severe deprivation with regard to material resources. And the provision of human resource development with respect to specific subject upgrading, while appropriate in itself, did little to help teachers while the educational system within which they worked remained in a state of chaos.

This example further highlights the problems created when services are provided which prescribe solutions with little regard for, or understanding of, developmental processes. Prescribed packages are a hindrance to, rather than a furtherance of, the development of a conscious, creative and human future. The practice of development demands a 'disciplined flexibility'.

A final example of development practice takes us into the realm of individual development. It concerns a development organisation which concentrated on economic development in a developing country where there was a high level of unemployment. In order to make its particular contribution, the organisation decided to target unemployed and unskilled people and develop their capacity to become self-employed entrepreneurs. It began by taking such people in off the streets and training them in the basics of a particular technical skill, such as leatherwork, butchery, sewing and so on. The belief was that people could become self-employed if they had a technical skill.

It took some time to realise that this was not happening; that the people who gained a minimum level of necessary skill to enable them to become self-employed tended to go back to seeking employment where there was none available and did not use what they had learned. Something more was clearly needed, so the organisation added an extra element into the training. For the first two weeks trainees were given input on the nature of trading and the business of making money.

They were also given a very small amount of money and told to increase it by the end of the two week period in any way they chose. Only those who had significantly increased their 'grant' were entitled to carry on to the next phase of training – the acquisition of technical skills.

This process worked to a certain extent, and the final results were slightly better. However, it was thought they were still not worth anywhere near the time and money being poured into the training. The qualities required of entrepreneurs were still missing when trainees finished their training. So over the following years a number of further elements were added to the training package. For instance, technical skills training modules were interspersed with short training inputs on business management, and on 'graduation' people were given 'start-up loans', and helped to manage their finances and repayments. The organisation also assisted its 'graduates' with the marketing of their products and provided the graduates with supervisors or mentors who visited them at their workplaces during a six month period following the training.

Still the results were thought to be insignificant. The percentage of graduates who managed to become viably self-employed, or who were able to earn even a basic living through their new-found trade, was estimated at under 10 per cent. The development organisation was encountering problems for three reasons. First, because it had become seduced by the number of graduates it was producing, regardless of their viability. Second, because with all these add-ons the organisation had become differentiated into many departments which tackled different aspects of the training separately and did not coordinate their efforts. Third, and most importantly, because the organisation was not working out of a developmental paradigm.

The idea was that if trainees received sufficient input they would be skilled and thus perform differently. However, turning unemployed and unskilled people into entrepreneurs was not a question of skill but of transformation, of development. Skills were a necessary component, but not necessarily of primary importance and certainly not sufficient. Trainees had to experience themselves differently: they had to develop confidence in themselves, in their abilities, and in their capacity to confront and manipulate a harsh environment; they had to overcome the years of socialisation which had conditioned them into a perception of themselves which was at odds with entrepreneurship; they had to become creative, courageous, proactive and had to take risks; they had to think of themselves as leaders rather than as followers; and they had to kindle enthusiasm. All this meant that they had to overcome their own resistance to change and their fear of losing the 'old' way of life in which they expected someone else to provide and complained when the provision was not forthcoming. They had to accept new responsibilities and challenges even before knowing quite what these would entail, and whether these would leave them better off than before. In other words, they had to move through all of the elements of the development process which have been outlined previously – particularly letting go of mind sets, fixed attitudes and ingrained habits as a way of 'taking on the new'.

This understanding entailed a major paradigm shift for the organisation and its practice. The concept of graduates was no longer applied to trainees who had completed training courses but was used only for trainees who had actually become entrepreneurs. The emphasis of the organisation's practice thus moved from focusing on the improvement of training courses to focusing directly on the developmental process of trainees. The organisation was entirely restructured so that departments could work symbiotically with each other in order to respond flexibly to the individual needs of trainees. And the process that trainees went through, apart from being more responsive to individual needs, was turned on its head. For instance, trainees had to begin their businesses at the start of the training period rather than on completion. This allowed the training to respond to their needs as they grappled with their environment, and it made the programme relevant to the trainees as they moved through points of crisis, change and learning on their path of development and transformation.

It would be wonderful to be able to detail the results of this transformation in development practice, but the example is too recent to say more than that it appears to be working admirably. Such a transformation requires an entire realignment of the organisation itself, and this takes time. It is clear that the organisation has found a new lease of life in its discovery of the key to both the problems and potential of its practice. Detailed results in terms of product will take some years to ascertain.

The key, however, lies in understanding the process of development, and adapting one's practice accordingly. The successful practice of the development practitioner is responsive, disciplined, flexible but constrained by the parameters of development itself.

Summary

The task of the development practitioner is to facilitate an increase in the power and consciousness of social groupings. Having said this, however, there are many different kinds of development practitioner, and the varieties of practice are eclectic. But this does not have to imply confusion and contradiction. We have underconceptualised development, and therefore development practice. An appreciation of development imposes an intelligent and intelligible framework on the variations of practice.

The particular role played by a development practitioner depends, for its relevance and success, on the particular phase of development being worked with. The attitude and practice which helps facilitate development at one stage often becomes detrimental at another.

During the phase of dependency development practice will consist in part of resource provision and activism. As independence is attained these are replaced by the facilitation of clients to come into their own power, and the building of organisational capacity and the provision of training. With the move to interdependence the role of the practitioner becomes the facilitation of the client's ability to self-reflect, self-regulate and to take conscious control of its own processes of improvement and learning.

Thus there is no single way to practice development. It takes time and energy; there is no end to the development process; and the relationship between practitioner and client is marked by shifts in attitudes and strategies. The practitioner needs fine powers of observation and the ability to interpret situations; the practice of development demands a 'disciplined flexibilty' responsive to, and constrained by, the parameters of development itself.

Interlude: Intervention

I had lost my cool and sworn at men I revered and at men who trusted me; men who were so much older and wiser than I. We sat now in an embarrassed silence, none of us quite knowing where to look. The weight of recrimination hung heavy in the air, though I realised that this came from me and was directed inwards. Their forgiveness went without saying; they were forgiving people. But I had overstepped a mark, and did not know whether I could forgive myself.

No sound broke the silence. The long room stretched away on either side of us, its edges lost in a twilight dimness. It was always twilight inside the shoe factory, cool and dark, a haven away from the harsh glare of the Wupperthal sun. Worn workbenches, generations old, lined the walls. Venerable tools lay where they had been left when the other men had gone to lunch. The smell of leather hung over everything, and half-finished shoes stood in rows, silent testimony to the perfection of craftsmanship.

Calling it the shoe factory was something of a misnomer. It was a workshop really, a place where craftsmen had worked slowly and painstakingly for over a century. Each of the four men sitting around me had been a shoemaker for at least 30 years. I valued their craft and their humble craftsmanship enormously. The shoe factory was my place of refuge; always welcoming, a place of brotherhood where time stretched endlessly and there was always space for a rambling conversation amidst the gentle tap of hammer on nail and the quiet clickety-clack of the sewing machines. Yet the shoe factory was also the place of my greatest doubt.

Development and organisational capacity had made modest headway in various spheres of Wupperthal life: the glove factory, consumers' cooperative, rooibos farmers' association, people's savings bank, residents' association. These developments were consolidating links between people, increasing their capacities and gradually generating the potential for a community of choice rather than one dependent on the whims of the church. But the shoe factory defied this pattern. The craftsmen refused to organise. Each individual shoe was the thing, not the factory itself. The shoemakers struggled with division of labour, with administration, with the constraints and complexities of demand and supply. They were simply not interested. They did not concern themselves with improving production, with competition, with the wider economic world with which they inevitably interacted. As a result, they had long ago ceased to make ends meet. The factory was totally dependent on the church subsidy. It had no resources with which to sustain or improve equipment. And the church was signalling that it could no longer afford to continue the subsidy. The shoe factory was under real threat of closure.

Every effort I made to facilitate a different consciousness met with failure. Somehow this very maintenance of traditional craftsmanship which eschewed the complexities and often meaningless activities contained in increasing specialisation and division of labour made the factory my haven. But I struggled to engender development.

The final straw which broke my cool had occurred over the previous few days. Faced with a massive order from a new client who promised to become a major buyer, the four men with whom I sat – and who together formed the backbone of the factory – had taken off to attend to their small rooibos plantations high in the mountains. It was not a case of alternative economic gain, for although the men battled to make a living their rooibos farming was not an economic venture. It was simply that, traditionally, they tended their fields at this time of year, regardless of other considerations.

My anger had known no bounds. Now I sat staring ahead of me aimlessly. Was I forcing something which had no place here? I had their interests at heart, yet I was pushing them beyond their own wishes. In the process I was destroying friendship and trust. Was it worth it? Was it, in any case, right, or developmental?

I stood up slowly, smiled at them wanly, and stumbled outside. The sudden move from shadow to light, the harsh glare of the midday sun, blinded me. I screwed up my eyes. Was I blinded by more than the sun? Was I blinded by my own need for developmental success, which overshadowed the reality of the four men inside? I no longer knew in which direction the path lay, nor where it led.

7

The Art of the
Development Practitioner

> ...O the mind, mind has mountains; cliffs of fall,
> frightful, sheer, no-man-fathomed. Hold them cheap
> may who ne'er hung there..."
>
> Gerard Manley Hopkins, *No worst, there is none*

The development practitioner engages in various and diverse approaches and strategies as part of development practice and in response to a careful reading of the developmental requirements at the time. These different practices include, as we have seen, elements of welfare work, of activism, of 'expert input' and advice-giving, of training, of project implementation, and of 'process consultation'. Some of these roles are not easy to reconcile. As lobbyist or activist, for example, one works didactically, attempting to impose change and influence policy, to mould the powers that be into an image of one's preferred paradigm. As process consultant, on the other hand, one withholds one's own preferences and attempts to get individuals and organisations to reflect, to become more conscious, to be able to perceive and work with different perspectives, to free themselves of preconceived paradigms, to make their own choices in maximum awareness.

These different roles call for different approaches, each of which has its own culture of practice associated with it. However, the development process itself is the manifestation and vehicle of the life force striving for greater consciousness. It is life's path on its journey of self-discovery. Intrinsic to this understanding lies a particular perspective to the approach of the development practitioner. The approach is quintessentially underpinned by the enabling of individuals and social groupings to challenge socially restricting paradigms and bring to birth new consciousness, creativity and responsibility in themselves. The development practitioner is primarily a facilitator of development in this sense. Thus, while called upon to perform a number of different roles, the core of the development practitioner's art lies in facilitation.

While the practitioner is called upon to analyse social context and to respond with the appropriate intervention, he or she must recognise that not all of these interventions are specifically developmental. Put slightly differently, although they may assist the developmental process, they are not necessarily, of themselves, developmental. Welfare work, for example, becomes detrimental when it begins to cause community dependency. Activist interventions towards changing unjust sociopolitical conditions may be necessary activities to liberate society so that development may take place, but they become detrimental to development when activists leave the people behind or when they become locked and blinkered in specific paradigms. Training interventions may be necessary to create amenable conditions for development but become detrimental when they are regarded as a panacea or as a solution for the process of development. The creation of an enabling environment may be necessary for development to be pursued, but the activities undertaken in this regard are not necessarily, in and of themselves, developmental. Facilitation is the core of the developmental intervention.

The art of the development practitioner is a subtle and sensitive one. It lies primarily in interventions which leave people better able to take control of their own life circumstances. It does not lie in doing things to people 'for their own good'. It does not lie in doing things to one set of people for the good of – on behalf of – another set. (Do not do unto others what they can do for themselves.) Development work implies finding the delicate and sensitive balance between intervening in people's lives – for any development activity is necessarily an intervention – in such a way that the intervention frees rather than imposes. Development cannot be created, it can only be nurtured.

Development work demands the highest form of consciousness from the practitioner, for it involves working with the creative tension generated by the conflict between the most polarised pair of opposites imaginable – intervention into people's lives on the one hand, and respect for the integrity and freedom of these same people on the other. Indeed, interventions for the sake of that freedom. Interventions which are intended to so assist people in their development that they render further interventions unnecessary. The ideal is fully conscious individuals who recognise their interdependence with others and with the world and who are able to act productively, responsibly and freely, balanced between a powerful sense of their own independence and the necessary recognition of the ramifications for others (and for the world) of their actions. Conscious people, for whom interventions are unnecessary. Yet we intervene to generate this state.

The essential tension between opposites generated by the intervention/freedom dichotomy reveals other conflicting polarities which need to be balanced in action: confronting and supporting, challenging and nurturing, 'doing to' and 'working with', patronising and unassuming, acting and listening, being understood and understanding. The art of facilitation lies in being able to combine polarities in interventions which increase freedom. Assuming responsibility for others in a manner which leaves people capable of acting for themselves.

Developmental facilitation as a professional discipline is an art rather than a science. For there are no rules, no regulations, no linear sequences of cause and effect, no real predictability. We cannot know whether a chosen intervention was the correct choice or not until we have actually made the intervention and observed the results. Confronting a leader with an example of his abuse of power may help him to appreciate better his role, or it may cause him to retreat from and resist change in a defensive reaction to a perceived threat. Perhaps a more supportive mode, understanding of the leader's anxieties and feelings of inadequacy, may have been more efficacious in helping him to move through his conventional knee-jerk reaction of denial. Perhaps not. Perhaps it would simply have confirmed him in current practice and not brought consciousness or changed practice at all.

The responsibility which lies on the development practitioner is immense, and there are no rules. But so with any art, for instance the art of writing. How do we know whether a sentence works or not? We have the technical guide of grammar, although even this can be bent. We have guidelines which assist: sentences need fluidity, a certain flowing fluency, yet simultaneously require a tension. Yet we never know if it works until we percieve its effect upon the reader. And readers differ, in ability and in taste. We need to approach development work with both temerity and humility, a certain awe and wonder. A tension between acting and remaining passive. How can we have the audacity to intervene in others' processes; yet how can we not? We know so little, we cannot predict. Yet we cannot walk away when the possibility of nurturing a struggling bud of development exists. Facilitation is, indeed, an art of a very high order, for it does not play with colour, or word, or sound. It interacts with people, it affects and is effected by people, and it therefore demands an attitude of utmost respect.

As development practitioners acting within the realm of civil society we must recognise the interplay between organisation and community, and between individual and organisation. A growing number of developing organisations implies a developing community, while the organisation cannot develop unless the individuals within it are developing. We need to be able to work directly with individuals, nurturing their growing awareness of themselves and assisting them to explore the discrepancies between conscious value and unconscious habit. How do we respond when a man who claims to be gender sensitive continually interrupts the women in a group by launching into diatribes on their behalf, and is unaware of his behaviour? Or when six regional directors of a national organisation tolerate without a murmur the incessant and presumptuous interruptions of the national director while gathered together in a meeting, yet refuse to acknowledge complaints about subtle forms of hierarchical behaviour being voiced by the more marginalised in the organisation? Perhaps individuals need to be helped to recognise and adapt their own behaviour patterns within the security of individual consultative sessions. Reflecting back to an entire group what seems to be happening may assist individuals to transform, or it may cause them to retreat. Either way, the group's development depends on the development of each individual. Some will need to become more assertive, others more sensitive. Some will require specific training, others to learn to put previous training aside. All must become more conscious.

With respect to organisations, an unending array of interventions is possible: skills training, structural adjustments, vision building, strategic planning, culture change, role clarification, teambuilding and conflict resolution, and evaluation and monitoring, amongst others. Many of these, however, while they may support development, may not in themselves be performed developmentally, and may in fact even be detrimental to the development process.

The developmental intervention is a specific form of intervention which, ideally, leaves the organisation capable of self-regulation without further intervention. It respects and encourages the organisation's own control over, and ownership of, the intervention, and it facilitates self-reflection, growing consciousness and awareness. It encourages reflection on action, both on those activities which are contained within the organisation as well as with respect to those which the organisation conducts towards the world around it.

External input which is not sought and owned by the organisation will not be taken into that organisation's conscious practice, and may in fact render the organisation more dependent. Certainly, the knowledge gained through both experience and theory, and brought to the organisation by the outside consultant, is essential and necessary input. Organisations cannot go it alone; they have need of specialist knowledge. But the developmental intervention will facilitate the organisation through a process of self-reflection to the point where it becomes conscious of its needs, capable of prioritising these needs, and competent not only to exercise control over inputs but to exercise ownership in the sense that the inputs are used constructively and proactively. The development practitioner, in facilitative practice, must always balance the nurturing of the process of self-reflection, of becoming conscious, with the necessary expertise and advice which he or she is able to bring.

I once saw a superlative tightrope artist in a circus; an exacting performer whose act was so demanding that his sweat poured visibly down into the circus ring below as he went through his paces – huge drops falling like rain through the air and landing with a muffled patter on the sawdust. The development practitioner whose mind does not slip with perspiration, if only metaphorically, is not struggling with a balancing act worthy of performance. The temptation, from the perspectives of both practitioner and client, is to opt for expert, fast answers rather than slow and challenging process work. Yet development, self-reflection and consciousness, is always primary; and expert input secondary. Because building the capacity to respond creatively is more effective than being given the answer to one discrete problem or set of problems. Indeed, answers are not necessarily convincing solutions in the first place; solutions can be said to have been effected when the organisation has changed, not simply when it has been presented with advice.

Yet of course facilitation is not simple, and I have at times provided expert organisational input prior to achieving adequate conscious understanding in an organisation. In order, in fact, to facilitate such conscious understanding. I once worked with an organisation which had made conscious many hitherto unconscious practices and norms, but which was stuck at the point of restructuring in order to support its new consciously chosen practices. Designing a new appropriate structure was not the main problem; making a final and complete break with old, divisive patterns was. I could envisage the necessary organisational design. I could also see that further development was unlikely until the organisation was actually living within the new structure, for this structure diminished the divisions between people which were the final block to completely honest and open organisational consciousness. (Divisions which were a function of the current structure and which hindered the final touches to an almost-finished common picture.) I cajoled and pleaded with them to accept a structure which I knew they were not yet quite ready for, and did not entirely understand. I asked them to trust my experience and expertise. It was a dangerous and difficult intervention, partly because I could well have been wrong and partly because I risked undermining the organisation's new-found integrity which was emerging through the development intervention.

In the event it worked, and with the new structure in place the final brushstrokes on the canvas were able to be put in place. Yet I have never felt happy about this intervention, and I relate the story for two reasons. First, to emphasise once again that balance does not mean compromise; that we cannot facilitate according to strict rules; and that there is no substitute for experience and particularly integrity – temptations called forth by the power of facilitation are sometimes highly seductive. Second, because I know from my own gut response, if from nothing else, that that particular intervention was not in itself developmental. Certainly, it assisted the development process; certainly, it took place as part of a large and longer developmental intervention. But in itself it was not a developmental intervention. I believe the distinction as I have drawn it is instructive, particularly if it causes the reader to reflect on his or her own practice, be it training, evaluation, research, funding, activism, or whatever. Not all social interventions are performed developmentally, and it is as well to be aware of the discrepancy between what one is actually doing and what one purports to be doing.

Individuals, organisations and social groupings are potentially highly creative beings, yet they slip easily into patterns which stagnate, paralyse, kill motivation and survive on superficiality. Our task is to ensure that they develop consciously. They are riven through with contradictions and blind spots, with hidden agendas and vested interests, with unconscious norms and habits, with practices whose implications are not fully thought through. And they change over time. They grow, take on different functions, face new challenges and tasks in a swiftly changing environment. Practices which were once correct become obsolete and destructive, innovations become routines, analysis and con-ceptualisation give way to assumption. We need to facilitate the working through of these issues in such a way that motivation, capacity, consciousness, an open and productive climate, ownership and control emerge. We need too to provide, and assist with the provision of, necessary inputs. But the development practitioner is not a deliverer of products, of easily quantifiable and packaged resources. Unfortunately, much that passes as development work today is precisely this. The provision of funding and buildings, clean water, health services, housing, technical advice, pre-packaged training courses. Necessary and worthy activities, they are not always delivered developmentally. Vigilance is required, not presumption. The development practitioner is involved primarily not with product delivery but with process facilitation.

The art of facilitation demands the utmost care. The practitioner is dealing intimately with living human beings engaged in what may be their most human, and humanising, activity. As such there is no substitute for respect and admiration towards the person or organisation struggling with the vicissitudes of becoming. We need to work with a certain awe and wonder for each unique path with which we are privileged to interact. It is important to recognise that any intervention, however well-intentioned or useful, is in some sense an intrusion, and a presumption. It is also necessary to realise that the value of the intervention will depend largely on its relevance and appropriateness for the particular place, or phase, that the client is in at that time. As development practitioners, then, we need to be able to 'read' development, and we need to be versatile enough to respond appropriately.

The art of facilitation begins with observation, which lies at the heart of a successful intervention. And the ability to really observe demands objectivity and therefore also a level of self-knowledge which will penetrate through to reality rather than simply reflect the practitioner's own confusions, assumptions or projections. We will, of course, need to interpret what we observe against a background of theory, knowledge and experience; the practitioner is valued precisely for this level of expertise. But there is a world of difference between imposing a grid of presumption onto a situation and distorting observation in favour of theoretical assumptions and rigidified experience, and an honest listening and observing which precedes judgement and which is then made more intelligent and useful through interpretation in terms of an understanding which itself is open to change. The tension between observation, interpretation and presumption is one of those tensions which must be maintained in conflict rather than compromised.

The development practitioner thus approaches developmental situations without preconceived agendas or mindsets. Rather with openness and the capacity and the willingness to really serve the best interests of the situation. The willingness to serve is the ability to withhold one's own will, for with service comes paying attention to the will of others. As Stephen Covey puts it, 'First try to understand, then to be understood.'[1] Examining our daily practice reveals how difficult this really is. Listening itself is an art, one which requires practice and skill and a tremendous amount of energy. Active listening, attempting to hear the underlying will of the other, is an exacting but very human activity. Scott Peck, indeed, defines love as 'paying attention', particularly to the developmental needs of others.[2] We must, literally, pay attention and attempt to pick up every nuance of a situation, its internal dynamics as well as its context, the forces which provide opportunity and forces which threaten. Competent observation is simultaneously focused and diffuse, precise and general, detailed and encompassing, specific and ambient.

Intervention, of course, is also an art and the second component of facilitation. Knowing what to do when, and how, in situations which are always ambiguous and unpredictable, and being able to adapt and use unforeseen consequences as further developmental possibilities, is nervewracking. It requires suppleness, balance and an innovative bent. Having the capacity to use different forms of innovation at different times, and to understand and work with the consequences of their use, is essential. Hard facilitation is confrontational and challenging, direct and often didactic. It can, at times, cut through the blockages caused by resistance and shock people awake into a self-reflective process, but it can also intervene too harshly into the integrity of other people's processes. It can cause the resistance blockage to harden into outright denial, and it almost invariably causes hurt. Soft facilitation is supportive and nurturing, respectful, unassuming. It relies on a drawing out, and the asking of questions.

Indeed, the primary activity of facilitation is the asking of questions. The ability to find and put the right question at the right time, the one question which will elicit further self-reflection and growing awareness, is a profound skill. Questions can also be used to confront and challenge, it depends on the nature and manner of question. Soft facilitation respects the development process; it is also, sometimes, unable to assist beyond a certain point if resistance to change or unconscious patterns maintain intransigence.

The art of facilitation is a dangerous one. It provides the development practitioner with immense power and ample opportunity to use that power. As such power can be abused, so it can also be simply misused. We are reliant on powers of observation and must make decisions about intervention in ambiguous and unpredictable situations. Under such conditions our own unconscious often gets in the way and clouds vision and action. For instance, how do I know when I perceive an unhealthy hierarchical pattern operating in an organisation that I am not projecting this perception onto the situation because I am unconsciously denying – or avoiding having to face up to – hierarchical dynamics in my own organisation? Or perhaps my recognition and pain concerning these dynamics back home are causing me to interpret other, unique, situations similarly? How do I know when I 'hear' a community's major need as being pre-school education, that I am not operating within a preconceived paradigm? How do I know when I intervene to diminish a potential conflict during an organisational intervention that I am doing the right thing and not responding from my own and deeply unconscious fear of conflict or confrontation?

The answer is I do not. The only manner in which I can minimise these possibilities is by engaging in my own process of self-development. I need to self-reflect honestly and critically; I need to develop consciousness, and to establish a healthy relationship between conscious and unconscious aspects of self. Development practitioners need to engage in rigorous and disciplined processes of self-development. That one should not expect of others what one does not expect of oneself is the least of it; the responsibility placed on the development practitioner demands it. Reflection on action, and adaptation of future action in response to that reflection, is the first prerequisite.

Development organisations must engage in their own development processes, but they should also provide opportunities and encouragement for their practitioners, and should demand rigour. How many development organisations provide adequate opportunities for their practitioners to receive critical and constructive feedback when they come in from the field, feedback which genuinely facilitates development? Yet reflecting on action is the most basic form of self-development.

There is another, more subtle, reason for self-development. This is the need to develop what may be referred to as 'inner resourcefulness'. It must be said again that, in development practice, there is no linear sequence of cause and effect, no real predictability. Under such conditions it is resourcefulness and creativity which are required of the practitioner. Lievegoed makes an interesting distinction between the concepts of efficiency and creativity. Efficiency, he says, is the endeavour to bring about a maximum effect with a minimum of effort, while creativity is the philosophy of the creation of what is surplus to requirement. Creativity requires more, not less, as is the objective with efficiency. He goes on, 'It will have to be said again and again that a lesson, a lecture, a therapy demands that one prepares oneself one hundred and twenty per cent in order that one can give fifty per cent in a concrete situation; which fifty per cent this will be is of course something that cannot be known beforehand.'[3] This in itself is a new way of thinking about the competence of the development practitioner as a social artist. Mere training will not suffice. Training will have to be supplemented and underscored by self-development processes which alone can provide the resources necessary for creativity.

The picture of the development practitioner as social artist needs to be complemented with the picture of the practitioner as fighter – as a guerilla fighter, operating from the hills, mobile and innovative, striking at the heart of unconscious social assumptions and presumptions. The development practitioner has to live outside the norm in order to question, doubt and challenge. In the final analysis, the development practitioner has only two resources on which to depend, and they are the resources of the social guerilla: inner resourcefulness and personal integrity. With these, the practitioner can maintain mobility in the struggle for social consciousness, unfettered by the ponderous weight of prevailing mindset or paradigm. The image was aptly expressed in the final verse of a song by Bob Dylan, written in the 1960s:

> All along the watchtower
> Princes kept a view
> While all their women came and went
> Barefoot servants too
>
> Outside in the cold distance
> A wild cat did growl
> Two riders were approaching
> And the wind began to howl.[4]

The two riders refer, in the song, to the Joker and the Thief, social outsiders who alone are able to question adequately and challenge the status quo, represented by the Princes, secure yet anxious and threatened on their watchtower, defending unconscious and unquestioned cultural norms which are obviously sexist and classist, amongst other things.

The issue is, really, that the abuse of power tends to thrive where consciousness is lacking, and the development practitioner is called upon – in the struggle to facilitate greater awareness – to challenge that power which has developed a vested interest in maintaining unconsciousness. The observation that power corrupts, and absolute power corrupts absolutely, is a direct expression of this phenomenon, a comment on how lack of consciousness operates. Corruption takes many forms, all of which thrive on an unconscious milieu. The social guerilla must operate from the hills, outside the norm, outside of the unconscious dynamic set up between the powerful and the powerless, on the side of the struggle for consciousness.

Two observations about power will assist in illustrating these points. The first is that power is never simply 'taken' by the powerful, but it is also 'given' by the powerless. Unconscious collaboration in a powerful dynamic which holds both sets of collaborators – the powerful and the powerless – in check is essential to the continued abuse of power. To break the pattern of abuse we need to break the dynamic of collaboration, and this implies consciousness. The second point is that power tends to coalesce into the centre, and the periphery tends to be marginalised. One can see this happening on a national level, where stakeholders tend to increase their hold on political, economic and cultural power to the detriment of those who are not 'players'. We see it in the rural/urban divide where resources tend to concentrate in urban areas and the rural are marginalised. We see it within urban areas where peri-urban squatters are dominated by the suburbs. We see it operating with respect to gender, with women being marginalised and men at the centre of power. I have seen it in community-based organisations where members – whose organisation it supposedly is – are marginalised and disempowered by elected office bearers who become manipulative stakeholders and a law unto themselves. I have seen it in development organisations where development practitioners on the periphery of the organisation – necessarily on the periphery as they form the link between the organisation and its clients[5] – are marginalised as power concentrates into the hands of a few at the centre, who pull the economic and political strings.

Wherever a development practitioner works, be it with development organisations, community organisations, social groupings or national institutions, if that practitioner is not working with the issues of the marginalised and developing consciousness by working through the unconscious hold of power which gravitates towards the centre, then he or she is not working developmentally. The essence of facilitation is helping to make conscious the unconscious dynamics which bind us.

It behoves us, then, as development practitioners, to be wary of the often so-called development solutions and options which emanate from the centres of power, be that centre the state, the North, the donor, capital, or transnational institutions which spin paradigmatic webs of international spread. As often as not, the plight of the marginalised is increased, and consciousness remains dim. Healthy development processes demand a strong civil society, and the proper placing for development practitioners is within the non-governmental sector. As an instrument of civil society, the development organisation is able to permeate, and be permeated by, the individuals and social groupings which it serves.

People-centred development demands interpenetration. The development organisation must be open to being effected by those whom it hopes to affect. Facilitation is above all a working together, a collaborative learning. If the development practitioner must develop through his or her own interventions then the development organisation must do similarly. Those who work to develop organisational consciousness cannot work from the centre. They must reside amongst the people, and work in partnership.

This concept of 'interpenetration' is a further manifestation of the development practitioner's art. The practitioner must be able to enter fully the client's reality, yet must simultaneously remain outside, capable of objectivity and of bringing something extra to bear on the situation. I recall standing one day in a hot desert town, conversing with a group of community members who were discussing a particularly thorny issue with respect to a development programme. The group was quite at home with the burning sun, the trickling sweat, droning flies, and the vernacular form of a language which confused me at the best of times. I was not, and I wanted the cool of shade and a tall drink. I remained outside the group and critical of the petty concerns which they raised, which seemed to obfuscate the real issues. But gradually I was drawn in, and began to realise that what I had thought were petty concerns were in fact real issues; that the conversation appeared to be going around in circles no longer bothered me as I was part of the circle. Yet, simultaneously, I was not. I was a development practitioner, not simply another member of that particular community. As such, I had to bring some 'added value' to the conversation, some objectivity, some insight or question which could break the circular flow of argument. But I could only do this from inside – I had to be inside and outside at the same time. And I had to recognise that what I had considered trivial issues were actually so real that the development programme itself might need to shift, not just the community.

That feeling of being part of a group yet watching it – and oneself – from a disembodied, outside perspective forms the very heart of the development practitioner's art.

Development practitioners, then, need the ability to be quiet, empty and respectful. Ultimately, however close we may come to understanding it, the process of development remains a mystery. Life is sacred, and the manner in which it strives to realise itself is veiled. People are an enigma. The attempt to penetrate the mystery can only be undertaken in the realisation that life and development remain forever beyond us and our capabilities. We need to approach them without presuming that we can master them, that our glib responses can penetrate to the heart. We cannot discover the secret. We can only hope that if we approach with reverence, with trust, with vulnerability and courage, the process of development will itself reveal its secrets, in its own ineffable unfolding.

Summary

At different times, under different circumstances, different forms of social intervention may be needed to engender development. While all of these interventions are necessary – according to the given context – not all of them are developmental in essence or are performed in a developmental fashion. Some may even be detrimental to the development process. The development practitioner must be able to diagnose context and respond appropriately. While the practitioner will need to perform various roles at various times – relief, lobbyist, activist, specialist – it is vital that the practitioner recognise the true nature of the art.

The art of the development practitioner is a subtle and sensitive one. It lies primarily in interventions which leave people better able to take control of their own life circumstances. It demands the highest form of consciousness, for it involves the balance of the polarities of intervention into people's lives on the one hand, and respect for the integrity and freedom of these same people on the other. Indeed, interventions for the sake of that freedom; assuming responsibility for others in a manner which leaves people capable of acting for themselves. And while there are concepts and standards which can support effective practice, there are no rules, no regulations, no linear sequences of cause and effect, no real predictability. Although hard interventions, specialist input, provision of services/resources, lobbying on behalf of others, are sometimes necessary, these interventions are seldom developmental in themselves. The development practitioner is involved primarily, not with product delivery, but with process facilitation. The ultimate objective is fully conscious individuals and organisations who recognise their interdependence with others and with the world and who are able to act productively, responsibly and freely; people and organisations able to meet the future creatively and freshly.

The art of facilitation demands acute powers of observation and the ability to self-reflect honestly on interventions. Because the power of the practitioner is immense, and because there is so much scope for projection of the practitioner's own unconscious, self-development processes are the most important form of practitioner training. The development practitioner is a social guerilla, striking at those places where consciousness is lacking and facilitating the growth of consciousness, for the breeding ground for abuse of power is lack of consciousness. Ultimately, practitioners' primary resources are their own inner resourcefulness and personal integrity.

Notes

Preface

1. Franz Schuurman, ed. *Beyond the Impasse: New Directions in Development Theory* (London: Zed, 1993).
2. D. Keet 'Systematic Destruction: IMF/World Bank Social Engineering in Africa', *Track Two* vol. 3, no. 1 (February 1994) pp. 10–11.
3. *Weekly Mail & Guardian*, 10 June 1994.
4. Wolfgang Sachs, ed. *The Development Dictionary: A Guide to Knowledge as Power* (Johannesburg: Witwatersrand University Press, 1992).
5. Vaclav Havel, *Disturbing the Peace*, translated by Paul Wilson (New York: Vintage, 1991).
6. Quoted in Theodore Schwenk, *Sensitive Chaos: The Creation of Flowing Forms in Water and Air,* translated by Olive Whicher and Johanne Wrigley (London: Rudolf Steiner, 1965) p. 98.
7. Vaclav Havel, *Speech to World Economic Forum* (Geneva: World Economic Forum, 1992).

1 Natural Processes

1. Dale B. Harris, *The Concept of Development* (Minneapolis: University of Minnesota Press, 1968).
2. Bernard C. J. Lievegoed, *The Developing Organisation* (London: Tavistock, 1973).
3. Leo Tolstoy, *War and Peace,* translated by L. & A. Maude (London: Oxford University Press, 1973).
4. Paul Davies, *The Cosmic Blueprint* (London: Penguin, 1995) p. 14.
5. See for example Ilya Prigogene, *From Being to Becoming: Time and Complexity in the Physical Sciences* (San Francisco: Freeman, 1980); also Robert Rosen, ed. *Theoretical Biology and Complexity* (New York: Academic Press, 1985); as well as Paul Davies, *The Cosmic Blueprint* (London: Penguin, 1995) and Margaret Wheatley, *Leadership and the New Science: Learning about*

Organisation from an Orderly Universe (San Francisco: Berret-Kohler, 1992).
6. Paul Davies, *The Cosmic Blueprint* (London: Penguin, 1995) p. 84.
7. Stephen Gould, *Wonderful Life* (London: Penguin, 1989).
8. Jacques Monod, *Chance and Necessity* (London: Collins, 1972).
9. Thomas S. Kuhn, *The Structure of Scientific Revolutions*, 2nd ed. (Chicago: University of Chicago Press, 1970).
10. Elizabeth Kubler-Ross, *On Death and Dying* (London: Routledge, 1973).
11. Max De Pree, *Leadership is an Art* (New York: Doubleday, 1989).
12. Quoted in 'De Profundis' by Oscar Wilde in *The Works of Oscar Wilde* (London: Spring, 1977).

2   Paths and Destinations

1. Paulo Freire, *Pedagogy of the Oppressed* (New York: Seabury, 1970).

3   Social Development as Growth and Revolution

1. Jan K. Coetzee, ed. *Development is for People* (Johannesburg: Macmillan, 1986).
2. See for example W. W. Rostow, *The Stages of Economic Growth* (Cambridge, Massachusetts: Cambridge University Press, 1960).
3. Elwil P. Buekes, 'Research Needs in Respect of Development in Southern Africa', in Jan K. Coetzee, ed. *Development is for People* (Johannesburg: Macmillan, 1986).
4. See, for example various articles in W. Sachs, ed. *The Development Dictionary: a Guide to Knowledge as Power* (Johannesburg: Witwatersrand University Press, 1992).
5. P. Streeton and S. J. Burki, 'Basic Needs: Some Issues' in *World Development*, vol. 6, no. 3 (1978).
6. Robert Chambers, *Rural Development: Putting the Last First* (New York: John Wiley, 1983).
7. Yvonne Muthien, 'Imperialism and Underdevelopment' in Jan K. Coetzee, ed. *Development is for People* (Johannesburg: Macmillan, 1986).
8. Peter Berger, *Pyramids of Sacrifice* (New York: Anchor, 1976).
9. Berger, *Pyramids*, p. 23.

10. This story was originally written for a CDRA publication entitled *Action Learning: Building Capacity for Development* (unpublished).

4 Development as the Building of Civil Society

1. Glyn Roberts, *Questioning Development* (United Kingdom: Acver Press, 1974) p. 14.
2. Howard Fast, *My Glorious Brothers* (Great Britain: Panther, 1960).
3. M. Scott Peck, *The Road Less Travelled* (London: Arrow, 1978) p. 305.
4. Berger, *Pyramids*.
5. Laurens van der Post, *A Far-off Place* (London: Penguin, 1974) p. 154.
6. Rainer Maria Rilke, 'Just as the Winged Energy of Delight' in *Rag and Bone Shop of the Heart*, translated by Robert Bly, James Hillman and Michael Meade (New York: Harper-Perennial, 1993) p. 236.
7. Monty Narsoo, 'Civil Society – A Contested Terrain' in *Work in Progress* no. 76. (July/August 1991) pp. 24–7.
8. 'Mission Statement of the Commmunity Development Resource Association' in CDRA Annual Report 1994/95 (Woodstock: CDRA, 1995) p. 33.
9. Berger, *Pyramids*, p. 236.
10. Frans Schuurman, ed. *Beyond the Impasse: New Directions in Development Theory* (London: Zed, 1993) p. 188.
11. Schuurman, *Beyond the Impasse*, p. 203.

5 A New Stance

1. I am indebted to Rabbi Hoffman of the Wynberg Reform Synagogue in Cape Town for this insight.
2. Robert Johnson, *The Fisher King and the Handless Maiden* (San Francisco: HarperCollins, 1993) p. 29.
3. Robert Bly, *Iron John* (New York: Addison Wesley, 1990) p. 209.
4. Bernard C. J. Lievegoed, *Towards the 21st Century* (Bristol: Steiner Press, 1979).
5. Ellen J. Langer, *Mindfulness* (London: Harvill, 1991).
6. Lievegoed, *Towards the 21st Century*.
7. Christopher Fry, *The Sleep of Prisoners* (London: Oxford University Press, 1960).

6   The Practice of the Development Practitioner

1. Sheldon Annis, 'Can Small-scale Development be a Large-scale Policy? The Case of Latin America' in *World Development*, vol. 15 (autumn 1987).
2. Piers Campbell, *Institutional Development: Basic Principles and Strategies* (Geneva: International Council of Voluntary Agencies, 1989) p. 5.

7   The Art of the Development Practitioner

1. Stephen Covey, *Seven Habits of Highly Effective People: Restoring the Character Ethic* (New York: Simon and Schuster, 1989) p. 53.
2. Scott Peck, *The Road Less Travelled,* p. 128.
3. Bernard C. J. Lievegoed, *Managing the Developing Organisation* (Oxford: Blackwell, 1969).
4. Bob Dylan, 'All Along the Watchtower'. Copyright 1968, reprinted by kind permission of Sony Music Publishers/Gallo Music Publishers.
5. See Alan Fowler 'Why is Managing Social Development Different' NGO Management Newsletter, no. 12 (International Council of Voluntary Agencies, Geneva, January–March) pp. 18–20 and L. David Brown and Jane Gibson Covey, 'Development Organisations and Organisation Development: Toward an Expanded Paradigm for Organisation Development', in *Research in Organisation Change and Development,* vol. 1, (1987) pp. 59–87.

Index

Index by Auriol Griffith-Jones